AF440021

Changing *Faces*

A Journey of Hope and Perseverance

Lisa D. Brown

Abuzz Press

Copyright © 2022 Lisa D. Brown

Print ISBN: 979-8-88531-074-1
Ebook ISBN: 979-8-88531-075-8

All rights reserved. No part of this publication may be reproduced, stored in a retrieval system, or transmitted in any form or by any means, electronic, mechanical, recording or otherwise, without the prior written permission of the author.

Scripture quotations are from The ESV* Bible (The Holy Bible, English Standard Version*), copyright © 2001 by Crossway, a publishing ministry of Good News Publishers. Used by permission. All rights reserved.

Full Cover and About the Author images by Monkey House Photography.

Published by Abuzz Press, Trenton, Georgia.

Printed on acid-free paper.

Abuzz Press
2022

First Edition

Library of Congress Cataloguing in Publication Data
Brown, Lisa D.
Changing Faces: A Journey of Hope and Perseverance by Lisa D. Brown
Library of Congress Control Number: 2022902599

Dedication

To my husband Steve, and two amazing boys, Logan and Landon: my life is blessed beyond measure with you. I love you with all of my heart, and thank you for supporting and believing in me through this endeavor.

To every parent raising a child with medical complexities and special needs: no prayer goes unheard. You are seen, heard, loved, understood, and never alone…even on your darkest days. God will equip you with all that you need to fight the good fight.

Contents

Chapter 1
Mayday! Mayday!

"Courage is not simply one of the virtues, but the form of every virtue at the testing point."

~ *C.S. Lewis*

January 18, 2002, 6:05 p.m.

The woman turned off the video camera. Tears welled in her eyes as she gently laid it down on my bed and walked out of the hospital room. The silence was suffocating, until my first newborn broke the sound barrier as he screamed at the world he had entered.

"6:05. You did it," uttered my husband with hesitation and confusion in his voice. Plans changed.

I looked at everyone, trying to figure out what happened. They looked around me with their reflected fear, masked with silence to the questions from my eyes. *Why isn't anyone saying anything? What happened?* Words finally formed, so I asked: "What's wrong? Is he okay?"

The room went dark. I was no longer in control. *Wait, did I even have control in the first place?* I was now aware of how sterile the room was. The fluorescent light above my head buzzed. The sudden urgency of the stifled medical staff in their muted scrubs and the silence of the other humans in the room swirled around me like a vortex.

This was the happiest and hardest day of my life. The cliché became my perfect juxtaposition. Nothing could prepare me for what life was about to be.

****

Chapter 2
Expect the Unexpected

"Never be afraid to trust an unknown future to a known God."
~ *Corrie Ten Boom*

Perfection. Isn't it the American dream? We want it all. We take necessary steps and make preparations for our lives with visions of what it will all look like for our future. For me, it was the house with a big backyard, two kids, and a dog, while it all works out perfectly according to our own dreams and plans.

I always wanted to be a mother, even as early as seven years old. I knew I would someday want to have a baby. Growing up, my little sister and I played house. We would stuff a pillow underneath our shirts and pretend we were moms-to-be. One year I got a Baby Alive for Christmas, which was the best present ever! I couldn't wait to hold it, feed it the little mush food that came with the doll, and even change its diaper. It's weird when you think about it. You put fake food into this plastic baby doll, then it would run through and out the other end. The gross stuff coming out of the baby, however, didn't matter to me. I carried it around anyway like it was real.

I imagined what the day would be like when my dream to have a baby became a reality. If it was a boy, he would look like his daddy and grow up playing sports in the backyard. If it was a girl, then she would have her daddy's eyes and my locks of curls. Subsequently, she wouldn't have to fret over her hair too much. Perhaps she would even love running track, like me.

After Steve and I dated a few months, we talked about things we wanted in life. "What do you dream of in life? Do you ever think about having children?" I asked.

"Yeah, I do want to have kids someday, a house of our own, and maybe find a church to go to," he replied sheepishly.

I was comforted and felt we were on the same page. "Good, I want those things too," I rejoiced.

****

January 18, 2002, 8:00 a.m.

Steve and I walked into the hospital to check-in. Inquietude veiled my demeanor for a moment, but I couldn't explain why. I chalked it up to nerves of giving birth for the first time and some fear of pain. Words of a labor instructor from a birthing class Steve and I attended three months prior, resounded in my ear, "expect the unexpected... expect the unexpected...expect the unexpected." She said this *three* times as she walked around the room while we were all on the floor pretending to give birth. I looked across the room where other pregnant women sat. It was so awkward I couldn't keep from giggling. We were all in a circle facing each other as we stared with uncomfortable gazes. It was a comical sight as the husbands sat behind the wives. I'm sure they all felt as awkward as we did.

Everyone breathed mantras of *he-he*, and *ho-ho*. I giggled more, which I knew embarrassed Steve because the rule was to be quiet. He was such a rule follower. The awkward silence made it even funnier to me.

After she finished her chant of redundant advice, I thought to myself *Lady, we get the picture.* For a split second, I wondered if this message was for me. I brushed it off, pretty much saying, "meh." I never told anyone of this feeling, not even my husband. Unbeknownst to me, God had already begun preparing me for His plan.

****

I can't believe I'm finally going to meet this little baby boy that's been growing inside me for nine months. I'm so excited to hold him when he comes out and see Steve hold his son for the first time. We sat and waited anxiously.

Both of our parents were arriving soon and we had the video camera ready so my mom could film part of the birth...from the head of my bed of course, no need for crotch shots.

Our family and friends started arriving, mingling in the room. Once my labor became more painful and intense, everyone left to go to the waiting room to anticipate the arrival of our baby boy.

After about five hours of labor-inducing medication, I had only dilated to one centimeter. Ten of course, was the goal. My pain from the contractions was severe now. It was as if a sword went straight through me from my lower back through to my stomach.

The anesthesiologist came in to give me my epidural. She had me lean over the side of the bed. "Okay, try not to move. I am going to insert a very long needle into your spine, and then after a few minutes you should feel relief."

I held onto the nurse who was standing in front of me. My inner dialogue argued. *Be still, she said. Kinda hard when it feels like my body is being twisted in half, but okay. I'll do the best I can.* So I did what she told me to do, through the pain, and remained hyper-focused on my breathing.

After yet another hour of agonizing contractions, it became unbearable. I kept repeating "this is not working... it's NOT working!"

"I'm going to go ahead and give you something to help you relax. It will not reduce your pain, but it might make you feel a little woozy," the nurse stated.

They kept giving me more drugs, simply putting me into a drug enforced stupor between the pains. Finally, I turned to Steve and whispered, "I feel like I am going to stop breathing, I don't want any more drugs."

The nurse who had been paging the anesthesiologist was getting frustrated with her. My nurse knew how much pain I was in since the epidural wasn't working. Writhing in pain with these cyclic matters, I finally asked Steve, "Please! Dig your fist into my lower back, it hurts so bad!"

"Okay, like this? I know you are in a lot of pain, but I am scared I will make it worse," he replied. He was trying the best he could but was a little freaked out.

"Yes, just make a ball with your fist and push it into my back as hard as you can. You won't hurt me," I pleaded. "This IS NOT WORKING!" I finally exclaimed.

Steve, who was about to blow a gasket, turned to the nurse. Before he could speak, she interjected, "I'm calling the anesthesiologist back right now. This is ridiculous. She shouldn't still be in pain after the epidural."

The anesthesiologist finally returned and asked, "So, you're still feeling pain, huh?"

Self-control, Lisa. Don't yell at her idiotic question.

I kept my wits about me and responded politely. "Yes, I am still feeling all the pain. Also, all these drugs I'm getting, knock me out in between contractions are making me feel like I may stop breathing," I said.

"Ok, let me remove this epidural and insert another one," she replied.

She requested I sit up on the edge of the bed again as she pulled out the epidural. My contractions had reached a number 10 for pain level at this point. Yet, I had to sit still and not move while she re-inserted it into my spine. It was a lot harder to be still this time, but I had to do what I had to do. As soon as she replaced the epidural, they laid me back down in bed. Voila! The agony exited my body with high velocity.

She had placed the needle into the wrong spacer in my spine the first time. I thanked God it didn't cause any damage to my spinal cord. I was still only dilated to a 1 at this point, but once my pain was under control, it only took about an hour for me to reach full dilation. Finally, I was ready to deliver this baby.

The hardest part was over, or so I thought. I pushed for almost two hours. *I don't understand why this baby won't come out. Is this a prediction for stubbornness?* I thought, jokingly. This baby boy was not having it. The doctor kept telling me the head was trying to come out, but retracting for some reason. They kept a good eye on monitoring the baby's heart rate and my blood pressure, determining whether to do a C-section.

"We'll give it a little longer with you pushing Lisa, but we may have to do a C-section," the doctor said.

"No, I don't want a C-section if I don't have to, I'll get this baby out."

At last, with a few more final pushes, I gave birth to my first 8lb, 4oz, 21in, long baby boy. He came out screaming at the world, which is always a good sign to hear the cry. I was happy to hear him cry. I think he was mad at me for making him come out of a warm and cozy place.

"6:05, you did it," Steve said. I fell back into the bed with relief. Time stood still. The room fell silent, all except for the baby boy who was still crying. He wasn't put onto my stomach like planned, and Steve wasn't offered to cut the cord as we requested. *Something's not right.*

I wasn't sure what it was, but I knew something wasn't good. I looked around at everyone's faces. No one was talking, or saying much of anything. There were only three words we heard: *it's a boy.*

"What's wrong, is he okay?" I asked.

"I'm going to go ahead and cut the cord down here, then we'll take him to the NICU and have some tests run," the doctor mumbled through his mask. "He has some syndrome-like features, so we need to make sure he is okay." Mic drop.

"Is he going to be okay? What do you mean, *syndrome-like* features? Does he have Down Syndrome?" I asked, all in one interrogative statement.

"Not necessarily Down Syndrome, but we're unsure what's going on. His head has an unusual bulge and his fingers and toes seem to be fused together," the doctor explained. Second mic-drop.

The room seemed to be closing in on me, almost like I was in a dark tunnel. Confusion was taunting me. I wanted him to be okay. *Was this a nightmare? Was this really happening? Is he even going live?* My body shook as if I was standing in an arctic blast, yet I wasn't cold.

"The shaking is a side effect from the epidural, and part may be from shock," stated the nurse's aide.

The nurse began pushing the button, calling for more help. "Hello?" Again. "Hello? We have a baby boy in room 308."

Within a couple minutes, a rotund nurse undulated into the room and hovered over our baby when she asked, "Dad, can you come over here please?"

Steve walked over to see him while they checked his vitals. I looked over to the side dresser mirror so I could see his reaction since I was still lying flat while the doctor stitched me up. I hadn't even seen my baby yet. *Maybe when Steve sees him everything will be okay. Maybe it's not as serious as it seems.*

Steve broke down and sobbed, creating an image, etched in my brain forever. This was the first time I had ever actually seen him cry. My heart broke into a thousand pieces. I felt I had failed him.

Questions were swirling around in my head like a tornado: *What happened? Where did I go wrong? It wasn't supposed to be like this.*

I was supposed to hold him, cuddle him, nurse him and everyone would go home like a normal, happy little family. It shouldn't be doom and gloom when you give birth. Tears of joy, perhaps, but not like this. I couldn't wrap my brain around the situation. Throughout my entire pregnancy, I ate the healthiest I had ever eaten and taken superb care of my body. *Why did this happen to my baby? Why is he suffering? Is this punishment for stupid things I've done in my past?*

My mom, who was at the head of my bed filming, turned off the video camera. Her voice shaking and crackling said, "I'm going to give y'all some alone time." She kissed my forehead, laid the camera down, and walked out of the room.

The nurses in their muted scrubs hustled around then brought him over to the side of my bed. He was all swaddled like a burrito in a white hospital blanket.

"Do you have a name for him?" the rotund nurse who was holding him asked.

"Logan," I said.

She asked a second question, "What about a middle name for him?"

I stared at his sweet squishy little face. *He was adorable. I saw a glimpse of his bulged forehead, but he was the sweetest sight to me.*

The nurse asked her question for a second time, "Do you have a middle name picked out for him?" she repeated.

"Huh?" I muttered as I snapped out of my twilight zone.

"Um, Wade... Logan Wade," I responded.

"Okay Mom, give him a kiss. We need to take him to the NICU now and start running tests," she said bluntly. She lowered his head to me. I kissed his soft and squishy forehead and got my first whiff of his scent. His sweet aroma made me want more of him. He was a precious sight and the most joyful scent I had ever smelled.

She scurried off to take my soft and squishy baby, who had *some kind of a syndrome*, to the NICU. I watched her as she scuttled off with the tiny being I carried for forty-one and a half weeks. The tiny being who kicked me while I would lie down and try to sleep. The being who made my stomach reverberate when he had the hiccups inside me. Panic slapped me in the face. My chest tightened. My brain finally began catching up, but catatonia hijacked my words, jailed them to the isolation of silence: *wait, please! Let me hold him first. Why can't I hold him? He needs to hear my voice. He needs to feel my touch. What if he thinks I abandoned him? Babies can sense their moms. What if he doesn't live and I never get to hold him?* But the words never left my mouth. I continued to question, *something*, somewhere along the way went awry, but *how?* My immediate knee jerk reaction was *guilt*.

The fact that this nurse asked me to say his name out loud forced me to focus on him, and not the nightmare I felt I was in. It was a small gesture, but a blessing nonetheless. This brief moment was validation that this tiny human was my baby, and this baby has a name. She could have easily rushed off to the NICU without batting an eyelash, especially since this was such a shock of unknown answers. Yet, she took a minute to normalize everything for me, bringing me back down to earth. I'm so thankful for her.

After my doctor finished up with my care, he walked over and sat on the edge of my bed and placed his hand over mine.

"I am so sorry," he said. My nurse walked up beside him with tears in her eyes, and they both were offering me condolences. "I'll be by tomorrow to check on you," the doctor finally said. He left the room.

"Would you like your family to come in now?" the nurse asked.

I looked at Steve. "Can we have a little bit of alone time first?" I asked.

"Sure, I'll go let your family know," she said.

Steve and I hugged for a long time, and then we cried.

"It's okay. It's not your fault… I love you," he whispered.

More nurses came in bringing medication and food. "Here is your pain medication. You should try to eat something too," one of them said.

"I'm really not hungry," I replied. I took my medication and was ready to see our family.

"You really should eat a little something to put on your stomach so the mediation won't make you sick," the nurse urged.

I obliged and nibbled on a roll. "I can't eat anymore right now," I pleaded. My appetite was void.

"We need to go ahead and move you to your regular room, but the NICU physician will be coming in soon to talk to both of you first," she stated.

The NICU physician came into our room with a very large, thick medical textbook. She started speculating the situation in which she named off two syndromes.

The first was Crouzon Syndrome and the second was Apert Syndrome. "I would lean toward Apert Syndrome, due to the appearance of his hands and feet. However, we need to wait until Monday for the geneticist to examine him and give an official diagnosis," the NICU physician explained. This meant two whole days of waiting and wondering.

"I found a journal article stating most children diagnosed with either Crouzon or Apert Syndrome *might* have an average IQ. But, there is a good possibility he will have mental retardation," she continued.

I couldn't help but run through the grocery list of "do's and don'ts" during pregnancy. *Did I miss taking a prenatal vitamin? Was it the old house we had lived in when I found out I was pregnant? Perhaps there was lead in the pipes or paint. Was it because I was too stressed out during the school year teaching kids with behavioral needs? Were there pesticides on any produce I ate during my pregnancy? Maybe it's because I had to take antibiotics during my eighth month due to bronchitis. Who knows if these are valid concerns, but what I do know is I have to stop this irrational madness in my head right now.*

"So he is going to be okay right?" I asked with a glimmer of hope.

"Possibly. We're doing every test we can. Again, this syndrome is very involved so you need to understand there is a chance of mental retardation," she repeated.

Okay doc, I know this is your disclaimer, but come on, throw me a freakin' bone here. My glass needs to be half full and I need some positive vibes here, so give me some hope.

"Steve, you should go talk to everyone now, I'm sure they're all worried. They will be taking me to another room soon anyway." I said as we tried to pull ourselves together.

"Yeah, I know. I'll be right back," he replied.

****

Chapter 3
This Wasn't Supposed to Happen

*"Your most profound and intimate experiences of worship will likely
be in your darkest days-when your heart is broken, when you feel
abandoned, when you're out of options, when the pain is great-and
you turn to God alone."*

~ Rick Warren

The Waiting Room

Steve's mom was standing right outside my hospital room with a friend of ours. They were both listening for the first cry.

A nurse approached them and barked, "Ladies, the doctor would not like you standing right here. Please return to the waiting room, and we will let you know as soon as the baby is born."

They walked back down the hall and sat in the waiting area. Suddenly, a nurse dashed down the hall with a baby all wrapped up.

"I hope that wasn't Logan," my mother-in-law proclaimed.

A couple minutes later, my mom came out of my room and walked over to the rest of the family. Through tears and a shaky voice she said, "Something isn't right. I don't think he has any hands or feet, but that's all I know."

A nurse walked over to my family and said, "The baby has some problems and the parents want to be alone for a little while. If you would like some privacy, there is a room over here you are welcome to wait in," she said. She took them to the private room. My mother-in-law sank down into a squat from her standing position, elbows on her knees. She placed her head in her hands and began crying. Everyone was quiet for a moment, not sure of what to say.

My mom spoke up and asked, her voice still shaking, "Can we pray?" They gathered around in a circle, held hands and prayed. My dad went weak at the knees and broke down and my father-in-law cried. Grief took over while they all held each other.

****

Steve left my room and walked to the waiting room to find our parents and give them the devastating news. He saw his parents first, standing in the hallway by some windows. They were calling other family members, friends, and their church pastor, letting them know what was going on, and to ask for prayers.

Steve approached them and began explaining Logan's physical features in great detail. He muttered through his tears, "Why did this happen? Lisa doesn't deserve this, I do. She hasn't done anything wrong. If God is mad at me, why did He have to take it out on Logan?"

"Son, God doesn't work that way. He isn't punishing you. He loves you so much. We are here for you, and God will help you through this," his parents reassured. They hugged and cried. "I need to go back. They will be moving her to a regular room soon," Steve said.

****

Time stood still, yet two hours had passed since I gave birth. It was finally time for me to hold my baby for the first time. My legs were still partially numb from the epidural, so I was happy when they pushed me in a wheelchair to the NICU.

The doctors had ordered X-rays, CT scans, and blood work of all of his organs. They didn't know his current health status, nor did they know his diagnosis. Once all of the tests were done, I was finally allowed to go hold him for the first time.

The nurse placed him in my arms. He was swaddled in a blanket. I snuggled with this warm new life and looked down at him, studying the *features* they described to me. *I don't care what they described; you're the most precious baby I've ever seen.* His forehead bulged and was soft and squishy. His eyes were wide open, bulging too, but so alert, staring back at me. Yes, he looked different. But I could not stop kissing him over and over, taking in his sweet scent, and talking to him. His alertness pulled me in, as if he was saying to me, "Mommy, I'm here, love me and I'll be okay."

This was our routine for the next two days. Steve and I would go down to the NICU to feed him, hold him, and rock him. His fingers were tightly fused at the tips of the bones. It looked like he was wearing skin mittens, sewn together at all the fingertips. His hands made somewhat of a triangular shape, the way they fused.

Then, something incredible happened. I slid my pinky finger up into the crevice of his tiny palm, formed into a tight, opaque cup, and I felt him squeeze, the best way he could! A floodgate opened as tears slid down my face. A sense of peace brushed over me, as I looked down at him while we were rocking in a rocking chair in the NICU. Through my tears, I spoke to him, "You're going to be okay. You are going to learn to do a lot of great things. I promise I will do everything I can to protect you and teach you. You're our angel baby."

Love brushed over me like a warm blanket. Divine love. I had no doubt in my mind of what my job was—to love, teach, and protect this boy with all of my being. I knew it was going to be a long road ahead. All logic pointed to stress… oh the stress. The dream didn't play out the way mine and Steve's had in our heads. But the love I felt was insurmountable enough to live this *new* dream we would be living now.

****

My sister. Goodness gracious, I've got to call my sister. We were two years and nine months apart in age. Even though she lived in another state, we remained very close. We talked on the phone all the time. She had also recently given birth to her first baby, a son, exactly four months prior. She had left a long distance calling number for me to use. This was back in the day before Smartphone, and it cost extra to dial long distance.

As soon as I heard her voice on the other line, mine trembled. I could barely get the words out. "There is something wrong with him, but they don't know what it is yet. His little fingers and toes are fused together. His head is bulging at the forehead. They are running a bunch of tests, so we should find out on Monday.

I could hear the tears through her voice. "I'm so sorry Lisa. One of your friends called to let me know. I wish I could be there with you," she trembled.

"I know Lori. It's okay. We can talk all the time and I will keep you posted on everything," I replied.

I made a couple more phone calls to friends, giving them my news. All I could muster were pragmatic explanations.

My brother came up that night to visit us. He had taken home the piece of paper that listed the two possible syndromes Logan might have. When he returned the next day, his voice was calm, reassuring… offering me more peace of mind.

"Lisa, I researched these syndromes. There isn't a whole lot of information, but from what I read, prognosis for kids with either of these syndromes seems pretty good, relatively speaking. He may have some problems, but there is a chance for leading a somewhat normal life in adulthood," he remarked.

I had my third affirmation of hope.

I stayed overnight in my regular room and knew the sting of reality was going to set in soon. It was going to hurt, but I needed to face it.

****

As nightfall came, I refused the sleeping pill. I didn't want to pass out with heavy drugs, only to wake up, thinking I had a nightmare. Everyone left to go home for the night, except Steve. He didn't leave my side.

The nurse brought an extra pillow, sheet, and blanket for him. He stretched out, *although I wouldn't call it stretching out*, on the vinyl sofa as it creaked. It was a perfect fit...for a child. He turned off the lights in the room.

I turned over in my hospital bed, lay on my side, and stared at the nighttime city through my window. The string lights ran down the side of the hospital building, glowing through my window. I could see downtown Fort Worth lit up with life in the near distance. Gravity of reality pushed me hard against the hospital bed. The quiet in the room coalesced my thoughts. I was at war in my brain, fighting the enemy who enjoyed taunting me with guilt, doubt, and fear.

I fought sleep and wished for the night to be over. My pillow became wet and the tears kept flowing. I grieved quietly through the night, for the dream Steve and I had for our son.

****

The next morning, my parents arrived while Steve was taking his turn to go down to the NICU and check on Logan. I hadn't even gotten out of bed yet.

"I don't understand any of this yet, but somehow I believe there is a reason and purpose for all this," I blubbered through my tears as they sat on the couch listening to me while I cried. There weren't a lot of words exchanged. They listened while I processed all of this out loud.

Steve walked back in the room. "It's your turn. They said there's a private room down the hallway from the NICU they're going to let you take him to and try to nurse him if you want," Steve said.

I anticipated this moment for nine months. My nature turned buoyant. *This is my chance… my first chance to do something good for him and show I am a good mom.*

My emotional hangover felt like a G-force, confining me to the hospital bed.

I sat on the edge of the bed, letting my legs dangle for a minute. I still had severe back pain and weakness in my legs, although, thankfully I could feel them. "I'm not sure if I can walk all the way," I professed.

"They left the wheelchair here, so you can ride in this," Steve replied, rolling it over to me.

"Oh, okay," I replied.

I slid off the bed while bracing myself on the mattress and allowed one foot to press against the cold, hard, hospital floor. *One more foot.* My second foot touched the floor, and then I sat down in the wheelchair. I wanted to move faster than my body allowed. I needed to hold my baby.

"I'll push you down there Lisa," my mom spoke up.

"That would be great Mom. I may need your help because I have no idea what I'm doing," I assured.

****

For the next couple of days, our routine consisted of Steve and me taking turns going to the NICU.

I sat in a gliding rocker to hold and feed Logan. He had a feeding tube dangling down from his nose, and tiny round stickers attached to wires intertwined, creating somewhat of a rat's nest of chaos to work around while holding him.

Oh how I wish you didn't have to go through this, Logan. We should be in our own home, comfortable and cozy. Instead, here we are in this room with depressing fluorescent lights, demanding beeps from the hospital monitors, and all the wires and tubes.

We had more friends and family visitors come to visit and hold Logan, except they all had to wait in a waiting room and come in only one at a time. Our sequestered space rendered anything but happiness.

I was discharged from the hospital on Sunday, but Logan was still in the NICU. He was moved from the one-baby NICU room, to the NICU with all the other babies.

They were kind enough to let Steve and me remain in one of the *stay-in* rooms for parents of NICU newborns. I felt pretty lucky to have had this room, because it helped me to feel a little less separated from him. Yet, isolation became my partner in crime. The room was small, dark and windowless, about one-third the size of a hotel room, just big enough for a standard bed, chair, and a bathroom.

I'm so thankful to be staying in here. We're so lucky to have been given this room.

****

There were about five other babies lined up around the perimeter of the walls in their incubators. Most of them were so tiny, presumably premature babies, clinging to life. I imagine I could have fit one of them in the palm of my hands. These tiny humans made my baby look like a giant. Of all my visits in that room, I only saw one set of parents. As I walked into the room, Logan was on the right, with two other incubator beds lined up to the left of him. Straight ahead was a young couple standing next to their baby. There was no eye contact with me, just them honed in on their sweet bundle of joy. The card stuck to the end of the incubator presented a print of pink baby feet. *I wonder if these young parents feel as insecure as we do right now.*

We never spoke with them. I was too engulfed in my own pain to think about reaching out to others. Small talk would be too exhausting, and I wasn't ready for it yet.

One more day until we would find out the prognosis. *Keep striving forward*, I kept telling myself.

Chapter 4
Diagnosis Revealed

"I sustain myself with the love of family."

~ *Maya Angelo*

January 21, 2002 - three days old

Monday morning, the whole family was summoned to a meeting with the geneticist. The room was barely big enough to fit Steve and me, much less both of our parents. We all sat in chairs anticipating the counseling session. She started out by confirming our son had a very rare condition called Apert Syndrome.

"This syndrome was discovered in the early 1900s by a man named Eugène Apert, pronounced *A-pear*, who was a French physician," she explained. She continued with a very detailed description followed with biological facts. "This is an autosomal dominant disorder. In other words, it is sporadic, which means it is a new mutation affecting the FGFR2 gene. Mom and Dad, neither of you are carriers of this gene. Approximately 1 in every 160,000 births is affected."

All the medical jargon became muffled, sounding like the teacher from the Peanut series, *wah-wah, wah wah wah wah,* until I was sucked back in by her next statement.

"This is a fluke mutation, it happens right after conception. It had nothing to do with what you did or did not do as parents. If you choose to have more children, your chances of having another child with Apert Syndrome are basically zero percent."

I pondered that word for a moment. *Fluke, she says.* The definition for the word fluke is *unlikely chance.* If you look for synonyms to the word fluke, you will find, *coincidence or accident.*

This was a scientific explanation instead of informing us they had no clue why this happened. There was no absolution, no reasoning, so it was even a mystery to them.

By the time I tuned back in to her speech, her words sucker-punched me right in the face. "He will need multiple surgeries to correct his skull, hands, and feet. He will never have a perfectly rounded skull like his dad's. But, they can do surgery and give his brain some room for growth," she explained.

My chest tightened again, as if someone had me in a restraint, making it hard for me to breathe.

How can this be? I sat there, astounded. Her words resounded again in my head like a loud gong... *multiple* surgeries. I wished I could take Logan home and pretend like none of this was happening. It was almost too much for my brain to process. Avoidance would be so much easier, but my reasoning knew better. I once read somewhere fear can be an acronym with two very different meanings: *Forget Everything and Run, or Face Everything and Rise.* I wanted to bolt out of there like a flash of lightning. But, I chose the latter.

****

The next meeting we had was with the social worker who assisted us with discharge paperwork, along with some resources. She referred us to the International Craniofacial Center at Medical City Hospital in Dallas. The paperwork included the medical itinerary of appointments, and we were to have two consecutive days in Dallas for tests, exams, and meetings, which would take place within the upcoming week.

Logan was discharged from the NICU, and we were given instructions for leaving the hospital.

"Dad, you go ahead and go get the car and pull up to the side of the hospital. There you will see a side door, and that is where you will pick up Mom and baby," the nurse instructed.

"Okay, I'll be right back," he said to me.

****

I walked next to the nurse who was pushing Logan in the infant hospital bed. She led us down a long, narrow hallway. There was nothing on the walls, and it seemed distant and empty, almost like this was some sort of escape path for emergencies. It was cold...so impersonal.

As we neared the glass door, I saw Steve parked on the side of the street at the curb. He got out and brought the infant car carrier seat inside so we could put Logan in it before taking him to the car. He's a winter baby, so I had two blankets to lay over him in the seat. The first one was a cozy, blue and white crocheted blanket my mom made for him with a matching hat. The second was from the Project Linus organization that the hospital gave him. It was quilted with a sea theme of whales swimming all around.

There was no celebration for graduating out of NICU, no hooray from nurses or staff. Instead, it was rather a neutral discharge out the side of the hospital building like we were being scurried away in secret and released to escape being captured from an enemy. Nonetheless, I'm actually glad there wasn't a big ordeal made when we were leaving the hospital because that would have only drawn attention to us.

We had one week to go home, try to lead a normal life in the meantime, and start preparing for the unknown. Nothing could prepare us for what was about to come.

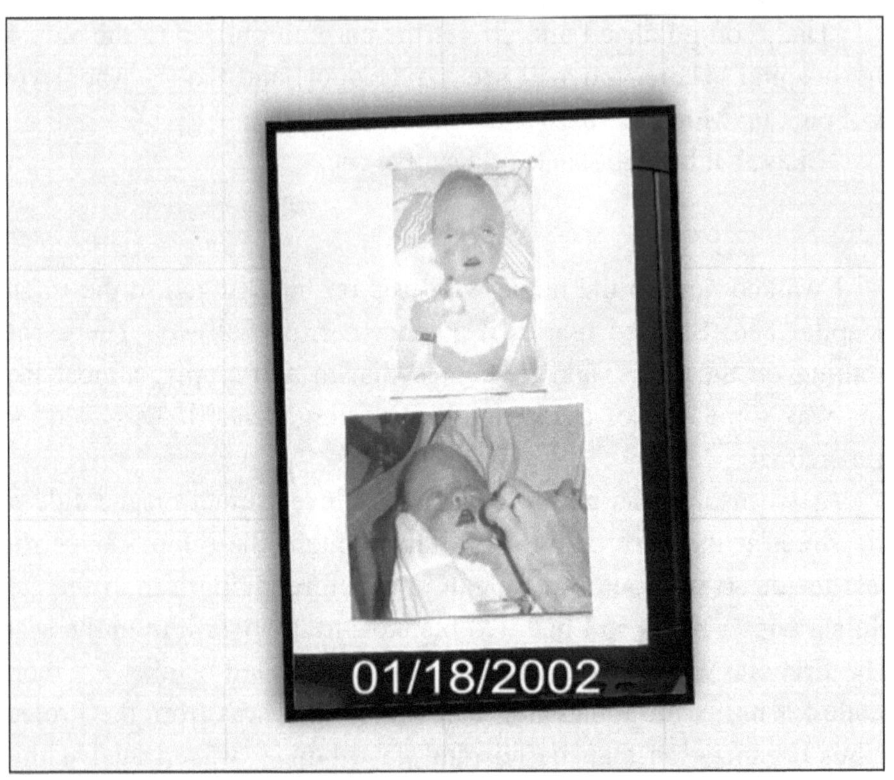

01/18/2002

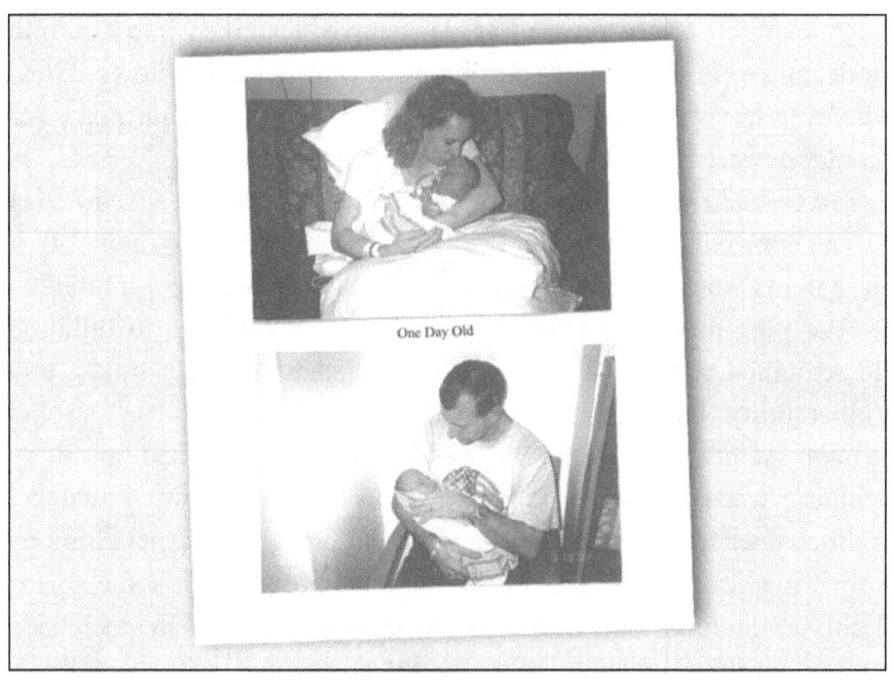

"...do not be anxious about anything, but in everything by prayer and supplication with thanksgiving let your requests be made known to God. And the peace of God, which surpasses all understanding will guard your hearts and your minds in Christ Jesus."

~ Philippians 4:6-7

****

Monday, January 28, 2002 - ten days old

The blood drained from my face as we entered one of the buildings at Medical City Dallas Hospital. It was as if we had landed in an airport in a foreign country without knowing its language. This hospital lived up to its name as a *city* with its enormous four buildings labeled: A, B, C, & D.

A twinge of pain pressed at my temple. I slipped into autopilot mode, allowing my mind to check out, and physically followed Steve wherever he walked. His steps were quick and with purpose. His shoulders were tense while his face was emotionless.

Steve had the itinerary listing all the appointments scheduled. It was an approximate two-hour drive from where we lived, and both of our parents were there with us the whole day for each appointment.

We ping-ponged throughout the day from building to building. He remained focused and driven as he led us through this… *city.* Vulnerability undulated around me like an aura as we strolled through the hospital. I kept my eyes on Logan as I pushed him in the stroller. I wasn't ready for potential stares or looks of pity. I switched my focus between Logan and the vivid pattern of the carpet along the wall. I memorized the pattern. It was dark brown with some sort of slight checkered pattern. It fancied a purple stripe on each side, outlining a long, rectangular shape down each break in the hallway. This became my runway, what I focused on while Logan was sleeping, and it was closest to the wall.

Every now and then I would look up at the walls I passed and saw large canvas paintings. They had thick paint, with a 3D effect. I could tell the artist used a palette knife to create the piece. They were a pleasant distraction. At least, long enough to take my mind off of the perfect storm we were heading into.

Our first appointment required Logan to have 3D CT scans under sedation. This meant no feedings for this little ten-day-old boy until after they finished. It was an unpleasant experience, to say the least. We handed him over to the radiologist while they took him into a room and put him under sedation to take the CT scans. CT imaging requires you to be immobile, thus requiring sedation for young children. Once they finished, they brought him out to me, then I found a place to feed him.

Our next appointment was with the anthropologist. For some reason I visualized anthropologists and archaeologists in the same profession - working and digging out in the field. Anthropology is the study of human biological and physiological characteristics. Seeing this team of medical professionals will be our annual routine until Logan becomes an adult. This anthropologist would track, make predictions, and chart growth progressions of his bones over time.

Well, okay then. Adding anthropologist to the list of team members. *Didn't see that one coming.* This was starting to feel a little like a scientific experiment. It all seemed so odd.

We proceeded up to the floor for our check-in. As we stepped off of the elevator, we walked straight into the waiting room. A tall, square pillar fish tank filled with colorful saltwater fish stood right in the center of the room. In the tank swam clown fish, lionfish, blue tangs, and others, all around a coral reef in the center of the tank.

To the right side of the waiting room were two sections. One was a play area for toddler sized children, and the other side had seats with a magazine rack and a TV mounted on the wall playing cartoons.

On the left side of the waiting room were two cubicles with open windows. A clerk sat on one side of the desk with a chair for the parent on the other. The sign on the counter was straight ahead. We walked up to the counter and they immediately knew who we were. They called for one of us to go over to the window cubicles to start the registration process.

Steve walked over to the registration booth and dug out his insurance card and driver's license. My dad and father-in-law were sitting in the waiting area to the left, right behind Steve. My mom and mother-in-law stood there with me while Logan lay in the baby stroller next to the lovely pillar fish tank. Then, it hit me.

I grasped onto the handle of the stroller and said, "This is *only* the beginning, isn't it?" not realizing I said it out loud.

"Yes it is," my mom replied with a shaky voice and tears welling.

I couldn't contain my emotions anymore. I broke down and sobbed. My mom and mother-in-law were crying with me, handing me tissues, trying to console me. The ebb and flow of emotions rushed over me like ocean waves crashing into the rocks of a cliff.

BOOM! *This is it.* BOOM! *My child is going to go through so much pain and suffering in his life.* BOOM! *Steve and I have to witness our son's sufferings when there is absolutely nothing we can do about it.* BOOM! *Will our marriage sustain through this?* BOOM! *This is now our life, and it's going to be hard. How will we ever get through this? How are we going to be able to afford any of this? Are there even any certainties? What happened to the unencumbered life he should have? This is so unfair!*

It was as if I was having an out-of-body experience. The voice of the nurse broke my reverie. "Logan," she pronounced as she opened the door to the waiting room. I collected myself, and then Steve and I followed the nurse back to the doctor's office. "Down this hall and to the right," she directed.

First, she asked me to lay Logan on a baby scale so she could get his weight. Then she took all his vitals and asked us so many questions. *How much is he feeding? How long is he feeding? Has he run any fever in the last twenty-four hours? How many diapers does he go through? How long does he sleep in between feedings? Is he currently on any medications?*

Next, she led us down the hall to another room where we met the anthropologist. He was a very kind, quiet, and reserved man. He pulled out a tray of some quite interesting tools, and began taking measurements of Logan's skull.

He proceeded by measuring his eye sockets, the bridge of his nose, nostrils, to the space between his eyes. He even took measurements of his feet. He recorded approximately one hundred different measurements, and then… that was it. No results, nor discussions.

We thought there might be some kind of fascinating findings or revelations he would discuss with us. Instead, we went back to the waiting room where we met with our family. The ladies at the front desk explained to us where we were to go next, which was in another building on the other side of this *medical city*. It was already so much to process and absorb. I was already wishing for the day to be over.

****

We headed off to go to the next appointment to see a geneticist who was part of the Dallas craniofacial team. Once again, I followed the patterns and tracks of the carpet, keeping my head and eyes down. I focused on Logan while he would sleep off and on, avoiding any eye contact with people we passed.

My heart swelled with joy and pain. Helplessness tried to consume me, filling my head with all the struggles this arduous life ahead of him would provide. He was the sweetest, most beautiful baby to me, but would others see this beauty? *Will the world ever understand how precious this life is? Will they shun him because he is different? Will the kids tease him because he looks different? Will he be bullied? Will I know how to take care of this fragile miracle with all his medical marvels and mysteries?* I couldn't bear the thought of him suffering or being in any pain. I wanted to take his place right then and there.

This sweet soul stared up at me with his big eyes, tiny face, skin-mitten hands, and squishy forehead. He smelled of lavender and baby powder, and he had no idea what he had waiting ahead of him.

I continued staring at him while I pushed the stroller. I looked up every once in a while, marveling at the colossal canvases on the hallway walls, lathered with thick paint and vibrant colors. One of them looked like a school of fish. Another painting we passed gained my attention. It was a portrait of a lady dressed in white, sitting by a trellis of foliage. She was sitting there posed, not smiling. Her expression was...aloof. It was almost as if she sat there, disliking the fact she was forced to pose for this portrait. I understood her grief. I too felt I was pushed into an uncomfortable situation I neither asked for, nor knew anything about.

I lifted my gaze and looked at people in passing, hoping to see some warmth, maybe a few cordial smiles. I remembered we were in a hospital and all the people looked somber. So, I chose to send a few smiles. Perhaps they were fake, but smiles nonetheless. I yearned for some in return.

Then, it happened. Some people rubbernecked like they were passing a wreck on the highway trying to see the crash. Others stared and looked away pretending not to see my baby. A few had scrunched eyebrows plastered on their faces. A twinge of anger pinched me. *I'm not ready for this.* The tamed beast inside of me awakened. What I wanted to do was look them in the eye and say, *"What is your problem? Why are you staring like that? I saw the face you made, and it was rude. Stop pretending you didn't wince when you saw my child, jerk."*

Instead, I focused my attention back and forth between Logan while he slept in the stroller and the canvases we passed. This was much safer anyway. The artwork didn't have eyes that wince.

And so it began.

****

Hurry Up and Wait

We had some time to kill before the next appointments, so we trekked down to the lobby. Bench seating lined a long half-bricked area filled with water fountains splashing upward and down into the tank in a constant flow. The wooden benches lined by the fountains looked inviting, so we camped there for a bit. I sat holding Logan in my arms. He was so relaxed. His eyes were wide open, fighting a nap, yet not fussy. I could tell the sound of the moving water captured his attention as he took in the serene sounds. He was so alert and staring around as if he was trying to find where it was coming from, taking it all in. I loved this moment capsulated in peace. I tried to shove all my fear and sadness out of my mind. I wanted to enjoy this moment, so I snuggled him, kissed his head, cheeks, and sweet little mitten hands.

The lobby looked somewhat like the center of a shopping mall. It had an open concept, stretching up three stories high. The open hallways on each floor were lined with planters filled with green foliage. Shops lined the perimeter providing food, a bakery, a convenience store, smoothie and sandwich bar, and a gift and flower shop. We strolled through the flower shop, looking at all the beautiful arrangements, gifts, stuffed animals and balloons. The distraction of the pretty things was nice for a moment.

A large metal water sculpture stood in front of the shops flowing over into a fountain and stretching out about thirty feet long with mini fountains spewing up from the water. Hundreds of coins glistened on the fountain floor.

Straight ahead were the main elevators to this building. To the right of the main floor was a beautifully designed, carpeted area with a colossal, faux, stationary carousel. It reminded me a bit of going to the amusement park as a kid, except this carousel wasn't only horses. Attached to the carousel stood vibrantly colored, carpeted animals for children to climb or sit on. An elephant, giraffe, snake, lion, rabbit, and a bear, each with a pole attached down the center of them for children to hang on for the imaginary ride. In the very center where the main pole attached was a giant tortoise with golden lights strung at the top attaching to each animal's pole. The space was inviting, warm and peaceful.

As our reprieve ended, it was time to head to our next appointment… the geneticist.

****

We made it to the next doctor's office and sat in the very small waiting room. A mom and son, about eight years old, were there waiting for their appointment. Her son, who appeared to have the same syndrome as Logan, played with a fine motor toy, manipulating beads from one side to another, twisting and turning like a roller coaster.

I watched him in awe, as he pushed the beads up and around the wire maze. My heart swelled with reassurance. He had kicked off his shoes, so I was also able to see his feet. His fingers and toes had a unique appearance to them, but I could tell, or assumed rather, he had had surgery to correct the fusion. He was functioning great and didn't seem to let his physical limitations get in his way. Hope glimmered in my soul.

The mom spoke up and introduced herself and her son. She shared with us that he did in fact have Apert Syndrome. I was still feeling timid, so we only shared a few sentences of small talk. Yet, I gleaned hope from merely witnessing her son in those couple of minutes in the waiting room. Everything *might* be okay.

"Brown family," they called, and all six of us walked back to a larger room to meet the geneticist. "I'm Dr. Day," he said, "Could I go ahead and hold him so I can assess him please?"

He held him in his lap and began singing to him while he was examining him. "How are you, how are you, how are you little one?" he sang. I felt my shoulders relax. His kind affections were a pleasant surprise.

When he finished, he handed Logan back to me and asked questions while completing a diagram of our family tree. He then drew a genealogical map, tracing our family history.

"Apert Syndrome is a *fluke* gene mutation that happens at conception," he explained.

There is that word again… fluke.

"This is not carried by either parent, unless the parent is already affected with Apert Syndrome," he continued. "At conception, when genes began mutating to create Logan's DNA, a specific gene did not match up correctly on chromosome 10q26. This is the gene which affects bone growth with his skull and face, and also fusing his fingers and toes. Logan does carry the gene, so he has a 50% chance of reproducing a child with Apert Syndrome. He will need multiple surgeries to correct his skull during growth. Furthermore, there is a more significant surgery he will need later on, to move his facial bones forward. This will protect his eyes and improve his breathing, which will need close monitoring with annual sleep studies," the doctor finished.

There is the *other* word again… *multiple* surgeries. My chest tightened again and I couldn't breathe.

I mustered up the only coping mechanism I could handle for the moment. Words my grandma would say resounded in my head: *"One day at a time, sweet Jesus."* I have fond memories of my grandmother saying these words. She loved Jesus and would always praise Him out loud. I was so grateful for those words, because Lord knows I desperately needed them.

****

The Grand Finale

We gathered up ourselves, and headed out the door for our last appointment. It was finally time to visit the craniofacial surgeon. We walked down the hallway to the next room.

On the outside of the door a plate said International Craniofacial and Cleft Lip & Palate Institute. We made our way inside to a very small and full waiting room with dark walls and track lighting. We checked in and I completed the pages and pages of paperwork.

"Logan Brown," we heard as the door opened. The sound of the door opening and the nurse calling his name caused me to jolt. Butterflies fluttered wildly in my stomach.

The head nurse took us all back to a small examination room, where we waited some more. The craniofacial surgeon walked into our examination room along with the neurosurgeon and about five other interns in white lab coats. We might as well have all been specimens in a Petri dish.

He introduced himself and asked if it was alright if his fellow surgeons in training could join us, which we agreed to. He explained Logan's diagnosis to them with his age and all our family history. "Mom and Dad, come on out here so I can show you as I explain my findings," he suggested.

Our parents stayed in the room with Logan while he took Steve and me out into the hallway where they had his 3D CT scans splayed out on the x-ray light boards. He spoke in medical terminology. I remember a weird term uttered - *severe kleeblattschadel skull, with multiple cranial suture closures.*

In other words, his skull was sort of in the shape of a cloverleaf to some extent, some of the most severe cases. Skull sutures are seams, remaining flexible for growth where the skull forms and connects, thus leaving a soft spot in the top center. His sutures fused prematurely, leaving no room for brain growth. The words followed by his explanation stunned me from all the medical mumbo-jumbo.

"We need to do immediate cranial surgery on Wednesday," the surgeon explained.

The metaphoric train I was trying to get on began moving faster. I now needed to start running to catch it. *Wait, what? Today was Monday, and he said surgery on Wednesday.*

"Wait, do you mean *this* Wednesday?" I blurted, completely mystified.

"Yes. There are stalactite points, or, bone fragments, growing toward his brain and need removing as soon as possible," he implored as he pointed them out. "We typically wait to do this surgery until approximately six months or so. However, these points could pierce and cause damage to his brain," he said fervently. "I will perform a CVR - a cranial vault reconstruction. We will use demineralized cadaver bone to build his forehead. We can shave down these points as well as release some skull sutures to give him more room for his brain."

Our focus shifted back to the 3D CT scans illuminating from the fluorescent lights. There it was. We stared at the black and white display of our son's skull on the wall. He pointed again, to what looked like little points coming down from the inside of his skull toward the brain.

The sight of the scans was indescribable. There were holes all throughout his skull, presenting as a porous slice of Swiss cheese. Big holes, little holes, some mimicking craters on the moon. It appeared there was no forehead bone.

My heart sank deep into my stomach and I felt sick. I fell apart right there in the middle of the hallway at the doctor's office while all the white coats surrounded us.

I felt Steve's arm slide around me as I sobbed. He was silent as he cried. Our parents cried. Even the nurses cried as they brought us tissues. I had my baby ten days ago, and now they're telling me they need to operate on his skull. Day after tomorrow they must *reconstruct* his skull!

This was my worst nightmare. They had prepared us for multiple surgeries, but I didn't realize it would be so soon, and the extent of it was inconceivable. *I haven't had enough time with him! I still had to sit on a donut pillow from giving birth for crying out loud. I'm not ready for this. We need more time to prepare. This is so unfair.*

I couldn't breathe. I struggled to catch my breath in between all my sobs, as the nurse manager and family surrounded us, trying to comfort the best they could, all the while needing comfort themselves.

All I could think about was the haunting fear of losing him. I'm supposed to be learning how to be a mom. I should be rocking my baby, feeding him, changing his diaper, singing to him, bathing him and snuggling him.

We will have to hand him over to strangers so they could perform the most horrendous surgery I had ever heard of. Ten days in this world wasn't even enough for me to conceive of the diagnosis, much less prepare for all this.

Before we left the doctor's office, they gave us a second itinerary full of pre-op appointments for the next day. We looked over the papers: *Registration; History and physical; Blood work; Media (pictures); Surgeon Appointment.* Go here. Go there. Do this. Do that. It would be a robotic day of emotional appointments.

****

The ride home was dismal. It was dark by the time we got back into our town since we had been in Dallas all day, and it was winter.

As my parents dropped us off, my dad broke the silence, "Lisa, we can drive y'all back to the hospital for the surgery on Wednesday. Let us know what time y'all have to be there and we will get here real early to drive y'all there."

"Okay, thanks Dad." I hugged my parents and we walked into our house. It was late by this time, so I fed Logan, changed his diaper, put some warm pajamas on him and laid him in the cradle next to our bed.

With news no parent wants to hear, Steve and I sat on the couch. Silent. Both of us emotionally drained, exhausted, and speechless.

Steve began making phone calls to his school district to let them know he needed to take some time off. He coached football, girls' softball, and taught Algebra. Luckily he was in between seasons for his two sports, but it was a call he dreaded. Taking a significant amount of time off as a coach was quite taboo, since he typically helped with other sports where needed. They were very understanding and told him to take as much time as he needed to take care of his family. I had begun my maternity leave, so I called my principal and a few friends to let them know what was happening. Steve's parents made phone calls to distant relatives as well as their church to begin a prayer chain.

We weren't sure how long the hospital stay would be, so we began making preparations by paying bills, packing a few bags for an uncertain amount of time, and making sure our dog Gracie was taken care of. All we knew to do was prepare for the worst, hope for the best, and pray hard.

Chapter 5
Brace For Impact

*"Whatever is going to happen, will happen whether
we worry or not."*

~ Unknown

We headed back to Medical City Dallas for pre-op appointments and went straight to the registration booth where they gave the three of us hospital bracelets to wear. We were informed he would need a blood transfusion. We had two options: We could opt for him to receive anonymously donated blood or take orders to a blood center to donate our own.

We both chose to donate our own, so we took the paperwork and searched for the nearest blood bank. Once we donated blood, they delivered it to the hospital and it was reserved for Logan. We had gone separate times so one of us could stay with Logan while we took care of this task.

I had donated blood before. It was no big deal and I knew what to expect, even though I despised needles. I drove to the blood center, walked inside and gave them the papers. They escorted me to a private room where they asked many questions about any international traveling, my personal life endeavors... *blah blah blah.* After the interrogation, they sat me in a lounge chair where the nurse prepped my arm. We made small talk, and then she stuck the needle in my arm. She stuck me a few times and I flinched thinking to myself, *lady that hurts! Find the vein already.* I hadn't realized tears were streaming down my cheeks.

The technician noticed the dismayed look on my face. She looked at me concerned and said, "Honey, I'm so sorry, are you alright?"

"Yes, I am fine," I replied, embarrassed. *At least from the needle sticks.* I didn't have the wherewithal to muster any explanation for my emotions. I wasn't crying from the sting of the needle, but the reminder of the trauma about to happen to my son and the contrasted simple needle poke had me thinking *ouch.* My emotions were attacking me. I laid back onto the chair and watched the blood drain from my arm. *Push down the emotions… suck it up and be strong for Logan and for Steve,* I told myself.

This was my first mistake. It wouldn't be until much later I learned how brushing my feelings under a rug, only creates clumps.

****

Pre-op Appointments

The worst part of the following day was hearing all the risks involved in the upcoming surgery. "He could have a bad reaction to anesthesia, blood loss, infection, brain damage, and of course, death. The risks apply to everyone, but I have performed hundreds of these surgeries," the doctor explained.

Still, those risks resonated with me and were downright frightening. Luckily this day was only a half of a day of appointments, which gave us a little time to debrief.

When we got home we began packing our bags for a hospital stay. I had no idea what to pack. *How much formula and bottles do I need? Don't forget the breast pump. Will the hospital provide baby items like diapers, wipes, bottles, formula? How long will we be in the hospital?*

I felt so unprepared because I didn't know *how* to prepare. The only thing I knew for sure was, I had had a baby, my son had a diagnosis of a rare syndrome I had never heard of, and I was learning how to be a mom.

Desolation and inadequacy enveloped me because I didn't know anyone else who experienced this… *Okay God, I am not sure why you trusted me with such a medically fragile baby, or why all of this is happening. I am as ordinary as they come. I am inexperienced, immature, flawed and an imperfect country bumpkin from a small town called Azle, Texas. I am really trying to not ask why, but it's hard, so please bear with me… and give me strength. I'm not sure if I'm up to this task.*

****

The Night Before Surgery

I gazed down at his sweet newborn face while I fed him. I fought the rumination of all those disturbing risks until I no longer had the capacity. Floodgates still opened allowing my unstoppable tears.

It occurred to me this sweet, innocent boy had no idea what was about to happen to him, but *I* did. It's what hurt me the most. Logic reminded me of the necessity for this surgery. I had no idea how this would pan out. I knew it would be painful, but I didn't know how much.

I continued to rock Logan in the rocking chair, and a large lump rose up in my throat. I began to pray...

God please protect my baby from all the risks mentioned. I'm so scared. I've never been so scared in my life. I don't know what to do. Help the doctors and give them steady hands. Please help Steve and me to make it through this together. Help us to stay strong, and not allow this to tear us apart or against each other. Please help my baby to live and be okay. Amen."

****

Time for Surgery

We had been up and down pretty much all night with feedings, but the alarm clock went off at 3 a.m. anyway. My parents picked us up and we left our house while it was still dark and arrived at the hospital at 6 a.m. to check-in for surgery. Steve's parents met us there. The nurses escorted us to the place they called the "holding room."

The large square room was divided into curtained sections with either cribs or gurneys, depending on the age of the child, and space for the parents. Nurses came in and out, taking vitals, and asking questions.

"Mom, go ahead and change him into this gown please," she said as she handed me a tiny infant hospital gown to put on him. It was soft and had whales printed on it. Then, we waited.

I sat in the rocking chair next to the crib, holding Logan and rocking him while Steve stood beside me. He was not allowed to breast feed or have any formula since 2 a.m. I felt so guilty I couldn't feed him.

He cried off and on, wanting his bottle. All I could do was talk to him, kiss him, and try to convince him he wanted a pacifier.

Mickey Mouse Clubhouse cartoons were playing on the Disney Channel on the small TV hooked to the wall.

The call came and all the butterflies in my stomach took flight again.

"Okay, they are ready to take you downstairs to surgery," the nurse informed us.

I looked at Steve, and saw pain in his expression. All the air I was holding in my lungs released. My heart beat hard and fast in my chest while my stomach twisted into a pretzel. I carried Logan as the nurse wheeled the empty hospital crib to the elevator, and Steve followed.

We were all led downstairs to the second floor where Steve and I were escorted into another holding room, and our parents to the waiting room.

I'm not sure what is intimidating about being in a hospital. It's an odd and uncomfortable feeling. *Is it the scrubs, the sterile smells, machines, fluorescent lights, or gurneys?* I visited hospitals numerous times as a kid because both of my maternal grandparents were often ill with heart disease and diabetes. I have memories of feeling a little scared at first as we entered the hospital to go visit them. Then it became no big deal. My sister and I actually made it fun. Mom would give us whatever change she had in her purse to go to the vending machine to buy a Coke and a snack. Back then, there was one very large waiting room with telephones on both sides of the room. We even got brave enough to take turns and answer incoming calls and call out the family names of the recipients, like we were receptionists.

Initial intimidation rushed through my veins again. So now here I am as an adult, with my own newborn child, not visiting, but awaiting this *cranial vault* procedure. Part of me wanted to take Logan and bolt out of there, pretending this wasn't happening. Logic intercepted.

Royal blue scrubs floated in and out of each patient's holding area. The nurses took vitals, asked questions, hooked up pulse oxygen machines, and double-checked the charts.

The anesthesiologist came first.

He asked us to explain our understanding of what was being done during surgery. Then, he asked all the questions: "When did he have anything to eat or drink last? Has anyone in either of your families ever had a reaction to anesthesia?

"I will be monitoring Logan carefully and managing his breathing. Do you have any questions for me?"

Steve and I shook our heads no.

"Okay, I will come see you after surgery."

Next, the surgeon walked up and said, "We are ready to take him back. Mom and Dad, do you have any questions?"

Steve and I stood there like a deer in headlights. We looked at each other, speechless. "No, I don't think so," Steve replied.

"All right, I'll see you after surgery."

The surgical nurse chimed in. "Ok Mom and Dad, time for kisses and goodbyes. I'll be carrying him back. We're going to take very good care of him," the nurse reassured us.

Steve kissed his head.

I showered his face and head with kisses and whispered, "I love you." I contained my next thoughts. *I'm so sorry you have to go through this. If I could take it away, I would.*

Reluctance paralyzed my arms, until I finally placed him in the arms of the nurse. She carried him down the hallway as the other nurse wheeled the empty hospital crib behind.

I watched her, this person I had never met until today, walk away with our baby in her arms, taking him to what I felt was doom. I didn't know if I would ever see him alive again.

I turned to Steve and swung my arms around his waist and buried my face in his chest until my sobs didn't come anymore. We cried together.

****

The surgery waiting room barely fit my family. Its chairs lined the perimeter of the room, with a small television mounted on the corner wall, playing a brand new TV show called American Idol. The jingle to this show was notable to say the least, yet a pleasant distraction.

After several hours into the surgery, a young lady came into the waiting room. She walked over to me and introduced herself and said she had a daughter who also had a craniofacial syndrome. I had no idea how she found out there was a newborn with Apert Syndrome having surgery in this hospital because I learned they were seeing a different craniofacial surgeon who was also in the same hospital.

She knelt down on her knees in front of me, and with a soft voice said, "I know how scary and overwhelming this is right now." She continued as she looked me straight in the eye and said, "God is going to take care of your little boy. He will help you and your husband through this. I will be praying for you all."

Her words embraced me like a gentle hug. It's like she knew I needed to hear them badly. Out of the corner of my eye, I saw her husband who was holding their daughter, waiting right outside by the doorway. She explained her daughter, who was about three years old, had surgery attaching her halo device (a term I vaguely remember hearing from the surgeon regarding a future surgery).

"We weren't sure if it would be too much for you to see right now," she continued. "He is standing there at the door with her," she stated.

I smiled and gestured to him with a kind wave.

She continued, "We have been discharged and will head back to our hometown in Colorado.

Wow. How incredibly hard it must be to have to travel for all these appointments and surgeries.

At the time, there weren't hardly any other craniofacial teams. I soon found out, there were families all over the world traveling here for this craniofacial team. We lived only two hours away. *How did we get so lucky? God sent this gentle lady to place her hands on my face, metaphorically lift it upward and kiss my forehead. He knew what I needed in that moment. She was my angel in disguise, and I didn't even think she knew it.*

****

Four grueling hours passed. The surgeon came through the door and my innards flipped like a pancake. We were anxious to hear the news.

"It was quite a challenging task, but Logan pulled through fine. He is definitely a fighter," he proclaimed. "They are waking him up, so you will be able to see him soon. I will be by to check on him in the morning," the doctor informed me.

A few moments later the PICU (pediatric intensive care unit) nurse came and got us. She led Steve and me to his PICU room, which had glass walls and a window to the outdoor world.

Steve and I walked into his room and there he was, our tiny, twelve-day-old baby boy, lying in his hospital crib. The entire top of his head was bandaged.

IVs plugged into each hand and taped to his skin. He had round lead stickers stuck all over his chest with wires going in every directing, monitoring his heart rate and pulse oxygen level. His eyes were swollen shut and looked like two small plums.

We both walked over to the side of his bed. Steve bent over and put his head down on the mattress and we sobbed together.

"Logan, Mommy and Daddy are here with you. You are going to be okay and we love you so much," I mustered with a shaky voice, since I knew Steve couldn't speak.

I gave him kisses and stroked his little arms. It was late in the afternoon at this point, so the room was dark with the last of the winter sun almost gone.

I placed my hand on Steve's back and whispered through a shaky voice, "God sure watched over him, didn't he?"

Steve could not speak. All he could do was nod his head in agreement. The tough, opinionated sports fanatic coach I married had no words.

As I looked up and saw the cold rain pitter pattered against the window, I couldn't help but wonder: *Is God crying with us? Does He feel as sad and hurt as we do right now?* I would take one hundred thousand knives to my body if I could take away all of this. It was hard to bear, seeing him like this, but we had no choice.

They asked us to keep the lights off in the room as much as possible. The brightness of the fluorescent lights could be bothersome to him. So, we functioned with the only light illuminating from the window of the nurse's station.

My senses heightened when I observed a CD player on the counter. A song titled "Rainbow Connection," from a lullaby CD by Kenny Loggins, played softly. I recognized it as a song Kermit the Frog sang. My heart ached.

I noticed over on the counter was a get well balloon tied around the neck of a plush puppy dog. The envelope said: "Logan Brown - PICU." The card had a comic sketch of a dad and mom with a baby in their lap that said: "…and baby makes three." I opened the card where it continued "…hours of sleep a night. Congratulations!"

The written message said: "Congrats on your new beautiful baby boy! He'll bring you more joy than you'll ever imagine! We're praying for you!" Signed by the sweet lady and her husband and daughter who visited us in the waiting room. With the card was a balloon tied around puppy named *Rescue. How gloriously appropriate.*

He spent about four days in the PICU. The International Craniofacial Institute had a reserved apartment about three miles away for families who travel. They were kind enough to allow us to stay in it along with our families.

I didn't want to leave the hospital. I wanted to stay up there, but they wouldn't allow me to stay in the ICU room with him. The nurses insisted that I leave and get rest because they monitor him around the clock and would call us if they needed us to come back up.

"Here is a direct number to the ICU nurse's desk. You can call any time throughout the night to check on him."

I didn't know what else to do, so I followed their orders, but guilt tugged at my heart. Steve drove us to the apartment with two bedrooms and a kitchenette. We made a trip to Target and bought an air mattress with sheets since both of our parents were staying with us. We were so thankful they agreed to stay. We needed to be surrounded by loved ones.

We settled in for the night. I got up in the night to pump my milk several times, but didn't call the hospital because I didn't want to wake my parents who were sleeping on the air mattress where the phone was.

After the sleepless night, I called the hospital first thing and spoke to the nurse.

"Hi, this is Lisa Brown, and I wanted to check on my son, Logan. How is he doing?"

"He's doing fine. He did have some apneic moments in the night, but he is fine," she explained.

Apneic moments. My lungs constricted, making it hard to breathe. *How could I have left him? I have to get to the hospital. He is so alone. Why did I agree to this?*

I'm sure I was making a mountain out of a molehill, but my urgency to get up there kick-started my engine.

"Steve, we have to leave, right now. I need to get up to the hospital."

We got everyone up, still in our clothes from the day before and headed back to the hospital.

As Steve drove the five-minute trip, it felt like we were a hundred miles away.

I wish he could drive faster, or rather take flight and land on the Careflight landing zone. I think my heart is going to jump out of my chest. Just breathe. Don't let this panic attack get the best of you.

The minute we got there, I raced to Logan's room, washed my hands and showered him with kisses. "I'm here, Logan. I'm not leaving again.

From then on, Steve and I slept in chairs at the hospital, until we were finally moved out of the PICU after four days.

It was so much more comfortable once we were moved to a regular room, and I could be with him the entire time. Steve and I were able to sleep on the small pull out sofa.

The floor nurse helped us get settled in our room and gave us a verbal tour of the floor.

"Just down the hall is the family kitchen. There's coffee, a refrigerator, and an ice machine. There's also a small utility room with a washer and dryer if you want to wash your clothes. Sometimes parents leave small containers with detergent when they're discharged, but if not, the gift shop downstairs sells them. Here's a scale and a chart, you'll need to weigh each diaper and mark it here along with the day and time so we keep track of his hydration and kidney function. On this other sheet, mark how many ounces of formula he is taking, also with the day and time," she finished.

"I am trying to nurse him, but he's been fed formula from a bottle after surgery. I am also pumping my milk," I informed her.

"Oh, I didn't know. That wasn't on your chart. Nursing moms should be getting meals from the cafeteria served to your room, I will make sure to set that up! You can store your pumped milk in the refrigerator down the hall. Just make sure to label it with your son's name and date."

"Okay, thank you so much."

So many things to do and remember. But, I will do as I am told. I'm so exhausted. Sleep deprivation is brutal.

Somehow, we made it through the next few days. Finally, we were discharged from the hospital. Home at last. I've never been more appreciative of our bed than now.

We received a lengthy letter from Steve's aunt that read:

February 1, 2002

Dear Steve and Lisa,

There are so many thoughts going through my head the last two weeks, hardly know where to begin.

But guess the best place is to say Congratulations on the birth of your son! Our hearts are joyous for you, yet ache for you as this little one has so many physical problems. But we know that God has given him to two parents who love him and will seek the best care for him.

Two years ago we received a Christmas card from a friend, who wrote about her grandson who was born with something wrong with his head and had to have surgery...time passed and we got back in touch. She explained that her grandson's head was quite large and forehead was pointed. At age 6 months he had surgery. Dr. removed front of skull, laid it out on a table and reconstructed it, put it back together with stainless steel wire and repositioned one eye. He is almost 3 now and is doing great.

When your mom called the next night to tell us of Logan's birth and told us about his head, I told her about my friend's grandson. My heart ached and you were on my mind and in our prayers constantly, but because of the friend's grandson, we had hope. We do not believe that was coincidence that we finally made contact with this friend after 2 years and on the day before Logan was born. Believe that was God's perfect timing.

On Wed., January 23rd, when I was reading the bible and the Daily Bread devotional, the scripture for that day was Jeremiah 18:1-10. I won't write it all out as you have a Bible and can read it. Know that this scripture is referring to the spiritual rebirth, but verse 4 jumped out at me and asked God to let me claim that verse for Logan: "And the vessel that he made of clay was marred in the hand of the potter, so he made it again into another vessel, as it seemed good to the potter to make." I cried and prayed for God to allow the doctor to reform Logan's little head and hands and feet.

We asked for prayer for Logan and all of you, at church, on the phone prayer tree, in Sunday School class and at Bible study. Your uncle sent email messages to family and friends in FL, TN, IN, IA, MO, KS, OK, MT, AND CA, asking for prayer for you all. I called Grandad's sister in IN and Mamaw's sister, Aunt Virginia (Ginna) in FL. Aunt Ginna asked her church and the ladies she plays cards with to pray for you. She called the 700 Club the night before Logan had surgery and a sweet lady prayed for him and all of you and asked aunt Ginna to let her know how Logan was doing after surgery.

Every time I talk to your mom or dad and hear a good report, we just thank God and praise Him for caring for Logan, you two, and all 4 grandparents.

All of our family is concerned and praying for you and keeping updated.

Love you all so very much,
Your Aunt

P.S. I enclosed a copy of a hymn called 'Have Thine Way, Lord,' that will continue to be my plea to God for Logan.

****

I was astonished after reading that we had so many people praying for Logan, and for us, many across the United States. It behooved me to write a letter back to his aunt, as well as to everyone else, including some pictures of Logan:

April 2002

Dear Family & Friends,

As some of you know, we had a beautiful son on January 18, 2002 at 6:05 p.m. His name is Logan Wade Brown, and he weighed a whopping 8 pounds 4.6 ounces and was 20 ½ inches long. He has blondish-brown hair, and beautiful deep brown eyes.

We wanted to take the opportunity to share our story about Logan with all of you. Many of you are already aware of his condition, but we wanted to personally tell you about him.

Logan was born with a condition called 'Apert Syndrome' which happened when two chromosomes did not connect properly when he was forming in the womb. His skull sutures were all fused together, which left his soft spot to be his forehead. His hands and toes are fused and webbed together as well. According to doctors, this syndrome typically is a cosmetic issue, and they told us that his brain and intelligence should be fine. Needless to say, this was quite a shock to the whole family. We were referred to Medical City Dallas Hospital to see a doctor names Dr. Kenneth Salyer, who is a craniofacial surgeon, and leads the International Craniofacial Institute. He is known all over the world for his work, and is considered the very best. He has been on TV many times, and people come from all over the U.S. and world to have him work on their children.

On Monday, January 28th, we went to Dallas to see Dr. Salyer for the first time, and he looked at the CAT scan of Logan's head and informed us that we needed to do cranial vault surgery on Wednesday, January 30th. They were very honest and told us that he was in the best of care, but that his surgery was going to be a complicated one. Although we knew he would be having this surgery, we were once again shocked as to how soon it needed to be done. Our baby boy was only 12 days old, and had his first cranial surgery. They decided to do the surgery immediately because the CAT scan showed that every skull suture had fused together, thus causing threat to his brain because there would be nowhere for it to grow properly. He also had some "bone spurs" as the doctors called them, growing down toward his brain, causing another threat.

On Wednesday, January 30th, Logan had cranial vault surgery for the frontal portion of his skull, which lasted many hours. He pulled through perfectly, and the doctors were very pleased as to how his surgery went, and they said he was a "fighter." He stayed in the Pediatric ICU for 4 days, and then got a regular room for 3 days. We finally came home on

February 6, 2002. Logan is doing and eating well. He now weighs 9 pounds and is 23 inches long.

In two months we will go back to see Dr. Salyer and schedule his second cranial vault surgery, to fix the back of his head. We are in the process of researching orthopedic doctors for his hands and feet, which will also need to be worked on between the age of 6-8 months old.

All in all, we are very fortunate to have a healthy baby boy, and we want to take this time to thank everyone for the flowers, food, support and most of all the continuing prayers. It means so much to us to have so many family members and friends who support us and care so much. Logan is cared for and prayed for, even by people whom we have never met. Words cannot begin to express the appreciation for all of this. We believe that everything is in God's hands, and we have faith in Him. He is the one that will see us through the good times and the rough times to follow.

Please keep the prayers coming, as we will pray for all of you. If you have access to the Internet, please feel free to visit the web site listed below that my brother created, which contain pictures of Logan when he was first born. We will try to update the pictures occasionally for you to see the changes after surgery, and watch our beautiful son grow.

God Bless,
Lisa, Steve & Logan Brown

****

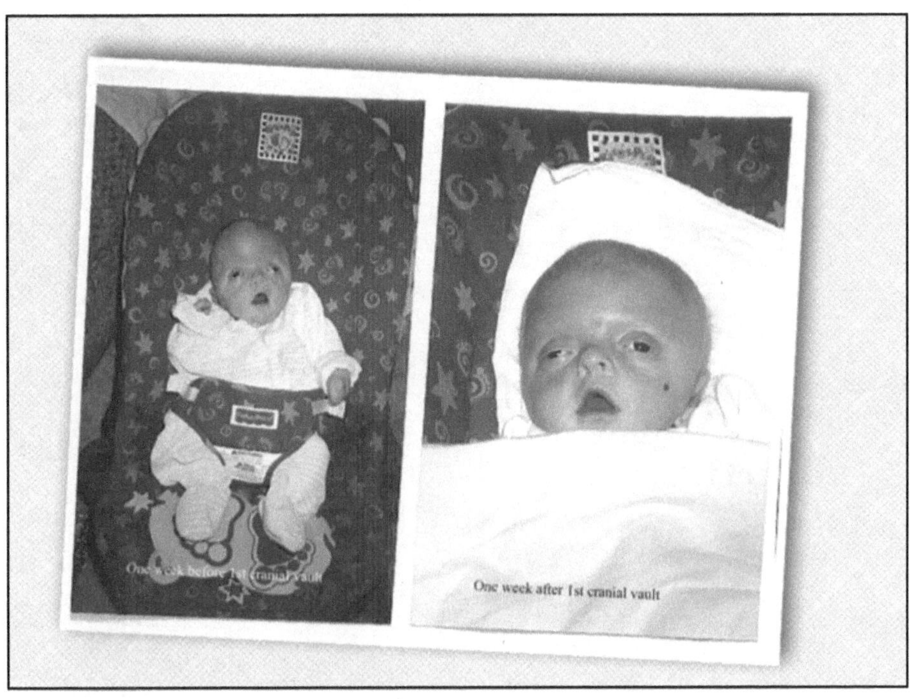
One week before 1st cranial vault
One week after 1st cranial vault

Chapter 6
Back Under Construction

"You've been blessed with a test."

~ *Melvin Bertram*

Five months passed, filled with recovery, new parenting, and joy. Finally, we felt a sense of normalcy… whatever normal was.

My favorite time with him was in the evenings. We kept a pretty structured routine, hoping to promote healing from the medical trauma. I gave him his bath, played music from two classical CD's my sister sent me, and lathered him in lavender lotion. Once he was dry and cozy, I clothed him in warm, soft, footed pajamas.

Logan grew accustomed to his bottle since he would not nurse anymore. We sat in the rocking chair and snuggled while he took his bottle. Steve and I quickly learned he loved when we rocked him to sleep after a feeding.

Developmental milestones felt like we had struck gold. At four months old, he learned to hold his head up. The most joy came one day when he did something extraordinary: He smiled and cooed. Knowing he was feeling happiness and love was all I needed.

****

One weekend we took a short two-hour road trip and visited Steve's parents. We decided to attend church with them on Sunday. Everyone there had prayed for Logan. This felt like a good opportunity to share all of our answered prayers.

As we were leaving, I buckled Logan in his baby carrier and sat next to him in the back seat. While everyone else was piling in the car, a man came out of the church and walked over to our car.

Steve's mom explained, "This is the man I was telling y'all about, the one who prays every day for Logan. His name is Melvin Bertram. He told us he prays for Logan."

He stuck his head in the window smiling, as Steve's parents introduced him to us. We exchanged hellos and then his next words resounded like church bells to my heart: "You've been blessed with a test" (1 Peter 4:12-14).

I expected questions of some sort about his diagnosis or even maybe some awkward moments of *I really don't know what to say* from him. I did not expect him to be so… forthright. To be honest, I had mixed emotions about it.

I didn't really grow up going to church often. I went a few times with friends and I once attended a church "lock-in." I learned a lot about Jesus from my grandma. My mom taught me children's bible songs like: *This little light of mine, I'm gonna let it shine.* My favorite part was: *Hide it under a bush? Oh NO!*

I also give both of them credit for teaching me how to say the simple child's prayer before a meal.

God is great. God is good. Let us thank Him for our food. Amen.

So, this message from this man had me befuddled. For months I replayed his words in my mind and over-analyzed his statement.

You've been blessed with a test? What does that even mean? Was it a polite way of saying: "Oh man, you've got work cut out for you." Was it his way of saying, "God is giving you a test, so you'd better study and do well, or else." Did it mean we were being punished? Did it mean we were "lucky"? I've never liked taking tests, so how can we be blessed with a test? Tests are hard. I'm an over-thinker, and am always one of the last ones to finish. It seemed like an oxymoron to me.

I even asked Steve, "What do you think he meant?"

"I'm not exactly sure," he replied, just as puzzled as I was.

Now I am even more confused. Steve grew up in church, and if he didn't know what he meant, then what now? I didn't know how to digest his statement. Yet, it left an unforgettable impression on me.

****

July 2, 2002

We settled into our routine of diapers, bottles, baths, bedtime stories, cuddles, rocking chairs, and sleepless nights for five months. Then, unfortunately, it was time to go back to see the surgeon. He summoned us back to the hospital to check on Logan's recovery and health status.

"His scar has healed well, so it's time to remodel the posterior (back) part of his skull now," the surgeon confirmed.

He had so many holes in his skull, it required them to add demineralized cadaver bone again. However, they wouldn't be able to fill them all.

We began the same routine preparing for his surgery. Pack our clothes, the diaper bag, get the house clean, make sure bills were paid, arrange for someone to take care of our dog...the list went on. I made sure I did not forget to pack his rescue puppy dog with us, and off to the hospital we went.

Approximately seven hours passed for this surgery. It seemed a little longer this time for some reason.

The anesthesiologist walked into the waiting room first. He knelt down beside our chairs running his hands through his hair.

"Logan came through the surgery well, but this was a tough one. He gave us a few scares. We had divine intervention on our side. He is definitely a fighter," he said.

After a long sigh, he ran his hand through his hair once more. "I'm glad he is doing well. I am off now, and I am going to go have a beer after this one," he stated.

Um...Ooooh-kay, I thought. I presumed something traumatic happened.

Next, the neurosurgeon came out. "Logan had several tears in his dura, which is the thin membrane lining surrounding the brain. I repaired them by stitching them up," he said matter-of-factly.

I don't know why this question immediately popped into my head, but I asked, "Will this cause seizures?"

"I'm not sure, only time will tell," answered the neurosurgeon. "He also has quite large ventricles, which are the areas where cerebrospinal fluid flows. We will need to keep an eye on that. If they fill with too much fluid, it can cause pressure on the brain. If it happens, then we would need to insert a shunt to continually drain the fluid," he added.

Finally, the craniofacial surgeon came out. "He's doing fine, and the nurses are getting him comfortable now in the ICU. I've placed a foam pad to the back of his head to keep the area stabilized. He will need to keep it on until the bone hardens. I'll check on him before I leave today," he said.

One of the nurses called us to go and see him. She gave our parents directions to a different waiting room for post surgery.

Steve and I walked into his room, only this time his eyes were not puffed up like little round purple plums. Nor were they swollen and stitched shut. His head was wrapped in white gauze with very thick foam padding inserted into the back. It looked as if he was wearing a turban.

"We will keep the foam padding in the back. The posterior (back) skull bones are soft with demineralized material. It needs time to heal and harden," the nurse reminded.

How on earth are we supposed to make sure he doesn't injure his head or turn wrong? So much could go wrong here…

****

By the third day in the PICU, they moved us to a regular room. It was the fourth of July and my mom bought Logan a new plush red, white and blue teddy bear, along with a small American flag on a stick.

"Steve, one of us has to try to sleep and there is only this *"chair-bed-thingy"* in here. I wonder if there's an empty room down the hall where you could lay down. The floor seems pretty quiet tonight."

"I don't know if I can go in a room and sleep there."

"Well I guess you could ask one of the nurses. They may tell you no, but it's certainly worth a try. You could leave and go find a hotel room I guess, but we don't have the money for a hotel."

"Yeah, I guess I will walk down to the end of the hall later tonight and see if there are any empty rooms."

I held Logan in my arms in the hospital room during the night, so he could rest his chest on my chest and take any pressure off the back of his head. I was so nervous I would bump his head or hurt him, but we sat in the chair and cuddled. Steve turned on the TV in our hospital room and we watched the fireworks show.

After a few days in the regular room, they gave us the discharge papers. We were ready to go home. We would rather have *sleepless* nights in our own beds.

Over the next several weeks, Logan slept in the cradle in our room next to my side of the bed. He had grown quite a bit and was a little too big for it, but I didn't care. I needed to be close to him and keep him as comfortable as possible.

He was still waking up needing a bottle during the night, and with all the bandages and foam on his head, it was too heavy for him to turn over in bed. I helped him get comfortable during the night and turned him over to his other side. After six weeks, we went back for postoperative visits and received good news he was healing well. Finally, time for a break... so we thought.

****

Third Time's a Charm...?

I would like to say life went back to the usual for us and everything was simple from then on, but it wasn't. We fell back into our routine. However, over the course of the next few months, we noticed a soft lump developing through one of the holes on the top of his skull. He also had a hard knot growing from the side of his skull on the forehead, which was there before his last surgery.

I placed a call to the doctor, describing the knot. The doctor's response to the hard knot: "that happens sometimes. The bone will grow in a different direction when it needs room."

Ummm, okay. So is that it? We let it be? It doesn't hurt him or cause injury to his brain? Why does it seem like I am the only one who thinks this is a serious matter?

What caused grave concern was when Logan woke up one-night crying. He was inconsolable. I did all the things we knew to do. I tried a bottle, changed his diaper, gave him gel for teething, and rocked in the rocking chair. I even gave him medicine for pain and drops for gas on the tummy. Yet, he still cried.

Although he had finally settled and fallen asleep, I felt it in my gut something was not right. I called the surgeon's office first thing the next morning and explained the situation and asked if we could bring him in. Steve's parents drove me to Dallas for the appointment because he couldn't get off from work. He was coaching football, and right in the middle of two-a-days. He worked a mandatory seven days a week, with four of the twelve hours each day in the one hundred degree Texas heat. It was taboo to even ask for a day off during football season. I was part of the coaches "widows club."

They squeezed in an appointment for us, then hit us with another blow of tragic news. "We have to open him back up right away because he needs more room. There is no room for his brain to grow, so it's trying to push up through the hole in his skull," the surgeon stated.

He was only seven months old now and about to go under the knife *again*, for *another* skull remodeling. I couldn't conceive of it! I thought we were finished with his head surgeries for a long time. I wrestled with confliction because I also understood the urgency. This news was like stepping on a rake when the handle hits you square in the face without any warning.

****

After we got back home, I went into our bedroom and called my mom to let her know the news. Mom was my safe zone. I knew I could spill my guts to her.

"Mom, I don't know if I can do this again," I sobbed as I told her he was going to have to have another cranial surgery.

"Oh Lisa," she said. I heard her on the other end crying with me, just as astounded as I was.

After we got off of the phone, I collected myself, and pushed it into high gear. I forced myself to accept the fact we had to hand over our baby to surgeons for the third time. Again, not knowing what the outcome would be. I still had to break the news to Steve when he got home.

****

Steve walked in the door that evening.

"Well, how was the doctor's appointment?" he asked.

"Let's go talk in the bedroom," I answered. We walked down the hallway to our bedroom and I closed the door. "The doctor said he needs another cranial vault. The lump on his head is his brain trying to push through because it has nowhere else to go. So, he said he needs to give him more room again," I uttered.

Steve stood staring at me, then finally broke his silence. "Did they say when?" he asked.

"Next week," I replied.

He let out a heavy sigh and rubbed his head with both hands. "Well, I guess I will have to see if they will let me have some time off. Not sure if they will or not, since it is football season," he said.

"Steve, surely they will understand and let you off for this, won't they?" I retorted. "I don't care what season it is, I need you there."

"You don't understand. As a coach, you *don't* take time off during football season. It's not that easy," he huffed.

"Well, this *is* kind of an emergency, don't you think?" I asked.

"I didn't say I wouldn't try, just don't hold your breath. You will have already used up all of your sick days for the whole school year, and then some. It's only the beginning of the school year and your paycheck will be docked. We don't need both of us to have docked pay. I'll ask, and let them know the situation, so we'll see," he answered.

You could cut the tension with a butter knife.

****

We knew the routine, what to do and what to expect, yet it didn't make it any easier. I think it is safe to say it almost made it harder *because* we knew what was coming and how hard it would be.

The swelling was pretty severe this time, making his sweet little eyes look like big plums. Nonetheless, this sweet boy endured his third cranial vault reconstruction (CVR) within seven months. He pulled through like the brave little trooper he was. He finally had plenty of room now in his skull for his brain growth and the lumps were gone. The only drawback was, so many holes still remained in his skull.

"We need to leave the holes since he is still growing. They are good indicators of any intracranial pressure," the surgeon stated.

****

****

At his six-week post-operation checkup, we learned his current craniofacial surgeon was going to be retiring soon. I felt panicked. *What do we do now? We were told this was THE doctor to see, the best of the best.* This surgeon was the one who was called in to perform emergency surgery when John Kennedy was shot in Dallas. *If he performed surgery on our former president, he must be good.*

We knew he would need another surgery soon to separate his fingers and toes. I wasn't sure what we would do, or who we would see. At the time, we weren't aware of any other specialists who were experienced with Apert Syndrome.

****

We were referred to another doctor who worked with the current team and had performed this specific surgery before so we made an appointment with him. While we were there, he examined his hands and felt around for his bones. Within about five minutes he explained to us he wasn't sure if he could give him all five of his fingers.

"The bones are there, but I can't guarantee I can give him all five digits. I can try, but since they are actually fused at the bone fingertips, there's no guarantee," he said.

Steve and I discussed this after we came home from the appointment. I really couldn't explain it, but something didn't feel right. I felt this doctor was haphazard with his examination and, rushed. I was not convinced this was the best option for our son.

We drove to the hospital for children called Scottish Rite Children's Hospital to get a second opinion. This time they took x-rays of his hands and feet. The orthopedic surgeon felt around on his hands and stated, "I could do a surgery to separate his fingers. I haven't performed this surgery before on any children with Apert Syndrome."

This was a fabulous hospital, yet we were a little discouraged. For some reason, Steve and I felt like we were not quite convinced yet. This was our baby, so we didn't take this life altering decision lightly. I wanted to feel completely confident in whoever was going to do this surgery. I also needed to know *they* were confident in giving us the best options for our child.

Doctor shopping was a whole new ballgame for us, and we never had to consider it until now. It was kind of like looking for a wedding dress, or a house… important and meaningful in life so you want to make sure not to be impulsive. You see so many, and there may be some you like, but you're just not sure. But, when you see it, you think *oh yeah, this is the one!*

I remembered the mom who visited me in the waiting room, the one who had knelt down and given me her encouraging words. She had mentioned the name of the doctor they were taking their daughter to for all of her surgeries, which were Apert related. She spoke highly of him, and had recommended we give him a visit if we ever needed another opinion or wanted to change doctors. He was directly down the hall from Logan's current team of doctors.

It was kind of strange, we hadn't heard of there being another craniofacial doctor when Logan was born, but what did we know? We went wherever they referred us.

She told us how pleased they were with the quality of care thus far, so we decided to give it a try. We picked up the x-rays from Scottish Rite hospital, and made an appointment to meet Dr. Fearon who gave us a *third* opinion.

He was such a nice doctor, very personable, and had a great bedside manner.

As he looked at the scans he said, "Wow, they did a fantastic job on these x-rays! All the bones are there and I can definitely give him all five of his fingers. This surgery is called a syndactyly release.

There are three types of bone fusion. There is type 1, which is the least severe, type 2, and type 3. Type 3 is the most severe and what we call *rosebud hands,* because the fusion is so tight. Logan has type 3, so it won't be easy, but I can do it," he reassured us.

A visceral sensation pulsed through me. After Steve and I talked it over, we felt we had our answer.

We went with our third choice, Dr. Jeffrey Fearon, whom we ended up switching to for his new craniofacial team—a choice we did not regret.

Chapter 7
A Baby Sea Turtle Has Hatched!

"If you can't fly then run, if you can't run then walk, if you can't walk then crawl, but whatever you do you have to keep moving forward."

~ Martin Luther King Jr.

Six weeks after Logan's third cranial vault repair, they put him on the schedule for surgery again. This time, they would begin releasing his fingers and toes.

The timing of this surgery was so he could begin developing his fine motor skills. He was already trying to hold his bottle, so I was excited for him to have some fingers loose. I wasn't thrilled with the process to get those fingers, though.

We took our usual trip back to Dallas for the pre-op appointment with the surgeon. "I'll be doing the syndactyly release in two separate surgeries," the doctor explained, "I'll have to take a skin graft from his groin area from each leg."

Logan's fingers were fused at the tips with skin and bone. With all four of the finger bones fused at the tips, it sort of made one giant finger, all covered with skin, as if he were wearing mittens. His toes were all straight forward, yet only fused with skin over them. I called them *baby doll feet.* They never separated in the womb so they needed skin grafts to place between the fingers and toes.

Beginning to prepare us for the recovery process for this syndactyly release surgery, the doctor explained, "He will be in casts on all fours, past the knees and elbows."

Sigh. Seriously? How in the world is this going to work?

He was just shy of being nine months old and sitting up on his own, learning to crawl to explore his world, and even trying to turn pages in a book with his little mitten hands.

I worried how helpless and frustrated he might feel, shackled with plaster for six to eight weeks. Quite frankly, perhaps the frustrated and helpless feelings would be more of mine to own than his.

We barely had enough time for our son to recover from his previous cranial surgery when we had to start planning for the next one. We were to the point where we didn't know if we were coming or going in life.

****

The day of the surgery came and we went through our usual song and dance. We were becoming experts at preparing for hospital visits by this point.

Thankfully, after about four and a half hours, the surgeon performed his magic yet again and the separation was a success.

Perspective is everything. I was so happy to not see his eyes swollen shut and a freshly scabbed S-shaped scar over his head from ear to ear. But, there was a trade-off.

When we got to see him, his tiny little arms and legs were encumbered in denim blue casts. They each had a *bend* for the elbows as well as the knees. All four casts had thick, foam rings wrapped around them at the ends. They were there to prop his limbs in an elevated position for proper blood circulation and reduce swelling. Relatively speaking, this was a much easier surgery. As for the recovery, that was a different story. He still had a lot of pain to deal with, as you can imagine how many nerve endings are at the end of your fingers and toes.

In addition to his four casts, I immediately noticed they had to place the IV in his scalp. This made for some treacherous and sleepless nights for him, and us. He still had all the leads and wires stuck to his chest. Since he didn't have any available fingers, they had to place the pulse oxygen lead on his little ear lobe.

This one little lead was the culprit of many nurse visits to our room. It would often slip off and cause the alarm to sound. This, however, did not compare to the mayhem I caused for a nurse one night.

It was the first night we were in a regular room. It pretty much goes without saying how exhausted we were at the end of the day. There was only one fold down chair in his room. It hardly fit me, much less both Steve and me. So, I told Steve to go home, I would stay the night. He could come back in the morning and bring me some *good* coffee. There was a family resource area offering coffee and a refrigerator for any cold snacks families wanted to store. The coffee wasn't the same as the gourmet sold downstairs, but beggars can't be choosers.

As expected, the night started out a little restless. First of all, I was trying to figure out how I could hold Logan and comfort him. That was a task in itself. I had to call the nurse when he would wake up so she could help me pick him up.

She helped me get to the chair and hold him without getting tangled in wires. He was heavy with all four casts, but the most difficult part was all the leads, wires, pulse oxygen wire and the IV in his scalp. I was terrified of moving the wrong way, or accidentally bumping it or causing it to come out. He was in enough pain, and he didn't need any more caused by me.

It was about midnight, so I decided to try and get an hour or two of sleep while Logan was sleeping. After I dozed off, it must have been about thirty minutes later when he woke up screaming and crying. I knew he couldn't be hungry because I had fed him a bottle right before I had the nurses help me get him back into bed. I changed his diaper, thinking it might be what was bothering him, but it wasn't a solution. I assumed he was in pain. It had been about three hours since his last pain medicine administration of Tylenol.

So, I got up and pushed the button for the nurse. I need to add, this night shift nurse who was assigned to Logan's room was about eight months pregnant. After I had pushed the button, she came running (actually waddling quickly) into the room, slightly out of breath. I know we looked at each other with puzzled looks on both of our faces.

"I think he is in pain, could he have some more medicine please?" I asked.

Before she left the room to go fetch the medication, she said, "I'll be back in a few minutes with his medicine."

I still felt a little puzzled. She came back a few moments later and gave him some medication.

I stood by his bedside for a while during the night, hunched over the bed rail with my head on his mattress, dozing off and on. He woke up so many times, I had to pick up his pacifier and put it back in his mouth every time it came out if he cried for it. He was definitely a pacifier kid. The problem for him with pacifiers was he had such a high, narrow, and thick palate. Despite him sucking on it, it wouldn't stay in his mouth. This often frustrated him, so he adapted by putting his bottom teeth over it to keep it in his mouth. Another indicator that this sweet boy would find a way to get what he needed.

This was my routine throughout the night. After a couple of hours, I became "zombified." I needed the nurse's help again. I wanted to lie in the chair with him on my chest to see if both of us could get more comfortable. I hit the nurse button, and she came running into the room again.

I looked at her sheepishly and realized what I had done.

I had pushed the "emergency" nurse button, setting off alarms at their station! Not once, but twice. *Oh crap. What is wrong with me? For the record, the button said, "nurse" on it. Sleep deprivation is evil.*

After the very pregnant nurse came running in again, out of breath asking if everything was okay, I hung my head in shame and replied, "Yes, I am so, so sorry," I replied mercifully.

She let out a sigh, then her voice lowered. "It's okay, hon," she lied. She helped me get him situated on my chest in the chair. She subtly handed me the bedside remote, the one with the *correct* nurse button. I felt terrible, but I was happy that my insomniac behavior did not throw her into preterm labor.

****

After a couple days of this routine, we finally got our golden ticket.

"The doctor signed your discharge papers. You are ready to go home," the nurse said.

Finally! We packed up everything and were waiting for the customary wagon ride exit with balloons and bags in tow. Off we went to go home and help our baby boy heal as best as possible.

The new challenge would be how he would take not being able to move and get around or pick up things or hold his bottle. What are we going to dress him in? It was October and starting to get cool outside. Even before this surgery, he had begun learning to crawl, which was like letting a little puppy out of a cage. He was so happy to be on the move so I felt so guilty he was again placed in shackles.

We entertained him with wagon rides, stacking cups for him to knock over and carrying him around on our hips.

I got quite the workout since those casts were heavy. He loved being on the move. After we got settled back home, I had to go back to work. We could not afford for either of us to miss work. I had already exhausted all my days off for the whole school year, and it was only October. We could not afford for my paycheck to be docked anymore.

Luckily, my mom and dad lived only about twenty minutes away and had agreed to keep him for me. So I drove him out to their house every day. They kept him entertained outdoors with tractor and wagon rides. He also loved taking his toy Hot Wheel cars and zooming them down the garden shed ramp. My dad often sat with Logan in his lap and turn on the computer synced to music with a visualizer. Little Logan fell asleep doing this so many times.

Many people don't have family to help, either because they still work, they have distant relationships, no relationship at all, or they are deceased. We were so fortunate that my parents lived close and were willing to help us out by keeping Logan while I went back to work.

****

One day, I was in a meeting with administrators, a speech therapist, and the parents of one of my students. The meeting was to discuss the child's progress he had made over the last school year in my class. My principal had a call come through to her office. It was my mom. "Lisa, it's your mom, you need to take this," she said.

My stomach flipped, because my mom never bothered me at work.

"Hi Mom."

"Lisa, Logan's cast on one of his arms has fallen off and everything is exposed. I don't know what to do!" she exclaimed with panic in her voice.

I looked at my principal, who had no idea what had happened, and without hesitation she said, "Go." So I calmly said to my mom, "Okay, I will be there in about twenty minutes. I will call the doctor to let them know I am on my way. Just stay calm."

I briskly hung up the phone, ran down to my classroom, grabbed my purse and headed out the door to my car. I called the surgeon's office on my way out to my mom's house. They informed me it was quite common for one or more of the cast to fall off, especially since his arms were so small at his age.

They asked me to bring him right in and they would put on another cast in their office. When I arrived at my parents' house, I walked in and my mom was holding him ready to go. I looked at his little hand, and between the fingers where they separated were black scabs and tons of stitches where they had sewn on the skin grafts. It was quite a gruesome sight.

We loaded into the car and headed to Dallas.

After a two hour drive and a ten minute doctor visit, a new denim blue cast was placed on his tiny arm.

My mom and laughed a little about the incident. We decided he was determined to get out of those casts one way or another. Darned if about three weeks later the little Houdini struck again! Another arm cast had slipped off. Although, this time it was near time for him to have the casts removed. So, they told me not to worry about bringing him in for another cast. Instead, we scheduled an appointment to have the others removed a few weeks later. He would be shackle free at last!

My mom went with me back to the hospital for his appointment to get all four casts removed. I have to say, the experience was a little traumatizing for all of us.

The technician used a device that looked like a small circular saw to cut through the plaster. Our nerves were strung as tight as violin strings, between the loud sawing noise and me having to hold him still so the cast was the only thing they sawed. Logan screamed and cried the entire time. I know he wasn't hurting him, but the noise was scaring him.

Stay calm and still… stay calm and still… This became my mantra. My irrational thoughts took over as I sat ruminating on my inner dialogue.

Please be careful. Mr. technician, please hurry up and get this over with! Oh, also, please don't accidentally cut off a limb, while you're at it.

Once it was all over, I put him in the stroller and we headed downstairs into the lobby. We had to wait for the next appointment so the surgeon could evaluate his hands.

Mom and I got some coffee, and we sat there chatting a bit, letting our nerves calm down. We were in awe as we watched Logan study his hands, turning them every which way. He was fully aware something was different. The look on his face was like he had discovered something new for the first time.

My mom and I looked at each other and practically said the same thing with a slight gasp in our voices. "He notices he has fingers now!" we both said.

I cherished this moment so much and wished I had my video camera with me. I knew he was really going to start exploring these little digits he now had. This moment provided joy and validation that this surgery was the right thing for him. He finally had some independence and freedom now to explore in more ways with his new little hands. I wanted to cry happy tears, but I denied the salty water from flowing down my cheeks.

Five More Fingers and Toes Coming Right Up!

Three months later, it was once again time to go back under the knife. His skin had healed up nicely where they took the skin graft. So, the doctor felt he was ready for the completion of his second syndactyly release.

Completion. This word was music to my ears. It was utter relief. He had recently turned a year old, so we were ready to get past this surgery. The good news was this surgery would hopefully be the last one for a good while. We were all ready to breathe a little.

****

He had about twelve weeks to recover when they scheduled him to go back again for this final syndactyly release. This time around, he had become a pro at crawling. We were a little more worried about how to entertain him this time with four casts on. Especially since it was winter. Usually winters in Texas are mild with temperatures ranging from 40s to the 70s. This year, of course, we had an unusually cold winter with a lot of ice and snow. Not conducive for outdoor wagon rides with casts and minimal clothing that fit over them.

Steve and I became very creative though, and yanked several tricks out of our hats. We pulled him around in the wagon inside our house. I bought soft white, cotton t-shirts a couple sizes too big to stretch over his head and slip his casts through the armholes.

Getting him into the car seat was quite a challenge too. I'm pretty sure I built some good arm muscles by this time lifting him and all four of his second set of heavy, purple casts.

So, he lived in oversized t-shirts and his diaper. We quickly realized how hard and rough his casts were. We bundled up thick socks to stretch over them so he would not hurt his head or face with them.

This little tyke decided nothing would stop him. Steve was taking a video of him when we realized he could still move in those heavy casts. We wanted to be sure to catch him in action on camera.

This kid is like the little engine that could. As I was lying on the floor with him, he decided to see me as a mountain, and instantaneously became a hiker. He proceeded to climb over me and then, *whack*! A purple, hard and scratchy cast struck me on the head like a bat to ball.

Ow! I saw a few stars for a couple of seconds, but I did not care. I turned and watched in awe as my son, who was in four casts above the knees and elbows, crawled away with a giggle. I couldn't believe his perseverance. It was a marvelous site.

We played the video back several times and laughed. You could hear when Steve blurted "Whoa!" when he saw Logan crawl over me and whack me in the head.

We're so glad to have captured this moment of tenacity. Needless to say, my head was sore for a few days, but man, how cool. I mean, who would have ever thought a one-year-old would be able to move this way, wearing casts on both arms and legs? Never underestimate the power of the strong-willed.

He crawled past Steve who was still filming and I noticed something. Right as he reached the linoleum tile in the kitchen I saw he had left track marks in the carpet. He reminded me of a little baby sea turtle who had hatched out of its egg, following his instinct to hike through the sand and find his way to its destination into the wide open ocean.

Logan was as determined as the little sea turtle, as if he had places to go and life to live.

For the next six weeks, he crawled everywhere with all four hefty casts on. Perseverance became his middle name. There's so much truth to the saying, "Where there's a will, there *is* a way."

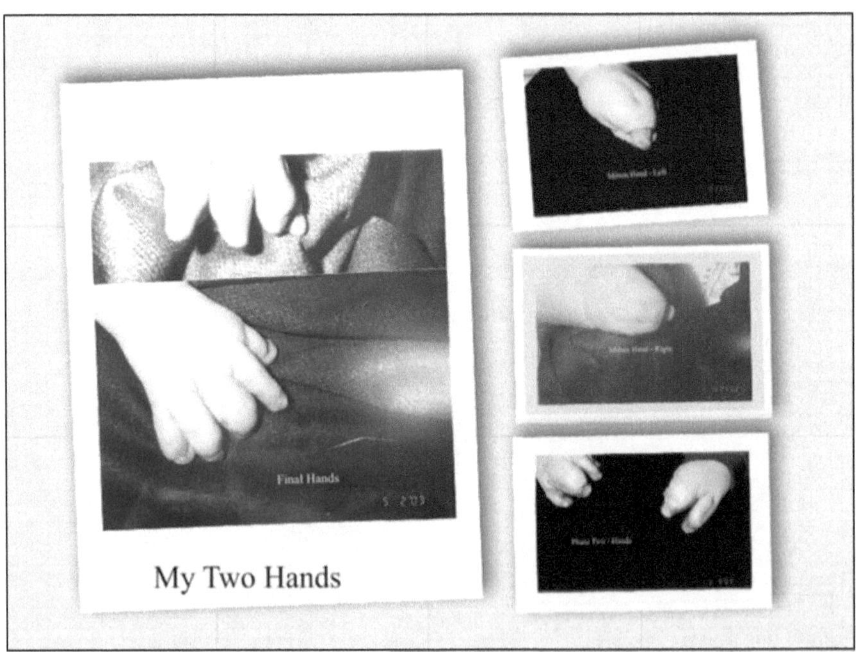
Final Hands
My Two Hands

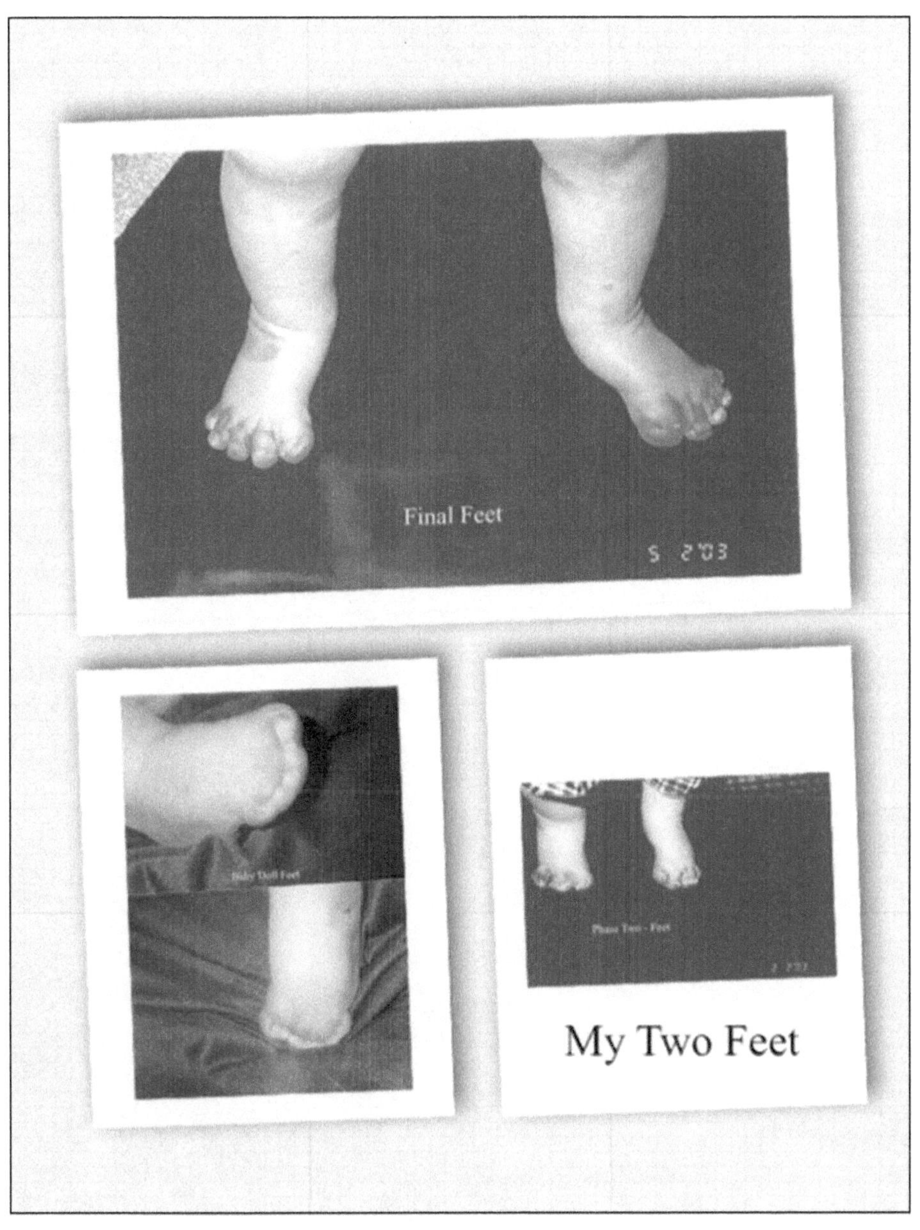

Final Feet
Baby Doll Feet
Phase Two - Feet
My Two Feet

Chapter 8
Happy First Birthday to Logan!

"Yesterday is history, tomorrow is a mystery, today is a gift of God, which is why we call it the present."

~ *Bil Keane*

It's party time!

One year, five surgeries, and thousands of prayers later, our son turned a year old. We celebrated by having family and a few friends over, sporting an Elmo themed cake and balloons.

Logan loved Elmo so much. He would be in another room and hear the beginning song of Elmo's World on the television and run to where it was playing.

He received many fun toys, including a special Radio Flyer wagon from Steve and me.

Sentiments surged through me as I placed the cake on Logan's high chair tray. The past year played before my eyes like a high speed slide show. So, before I turned into a blubbering idiot, I asked everyone to sing.

"Ok everybody, we're going to sing real fast," I said.

The truth is, I *was* in a hurry to get past the birthday song. I wasn't ready yet to let go of the feelings harbored in place in the back of my mind, nestled quietly. People are happy when they sing, so why not hasten?

After all...

One year ago, God blessed us with a bundle of joy who has already taught us about perseverance, strength, and most importantly, love.

One year ago, we received a diagnosis none of us had ever heard of.

One year ago, we didn't know if he would walk or talk.

One year ago, we didn't know if he would live.

One year later, he is still here with us.

God answered our prayers.

After the birthday presents were opened, the cake was eaten, and chaos settled, I took some time in the evening and reflected over the past year. It was astonishing at what we had overcome as a family, and how many answered prayers we had.

I had a baby...my baby has a diagnosis.

My baby has had five surgeries. Five. That's more than most adults will have in their lifetime.

We are still married.

We are broke, but not broken yet.

Thank goodness for photos and videos. Year One almost seemed like a blur since so much had happened. We still have so much to look forward to and so much to learn. We experienced miracles, and I knew God was my teacher.

Now, it's time to get busy living.

The Lost Number

I finally felt like we were in the clear from surgeries for a while. One day I searched for the piece of paper with the phone number and email address of the sweet mom who had taken the time to speak to us during Logan's very first surgery. I wanted her to know how much her encouragement meant to us.

I tore my house apart looking for the piece of paper, but never found it.

My heart sank. Somehow, it got lost during our discharge from the hospital.

I wanted to thank her for so many reasons, but most importantly, for taking time during her own daughter's recovery to reach out to us. Her face-to-face encouragement made an impact on me.

I also wanted her to know I understood how hard it might have been, not knowing what to say to others who are going through tough times, especially if they are strangers. Everyone responds to trauma in different ways.

I often wonder if she was ever hesitant, or second-guessing whether or not to enter the surgery waiting room. Did she have questions like *What if this makes them uncomfortable? What if I say the wrong thing?* More importantly, I wanted to know how her daughter was doing, how they were doing as a family. I craved her words of wisdom.

I hoped to connect with her again someday.

****

Children's Craniofacial Association

After one of Logan's surgeries during his first year, we were connected with the Children's Craniofacial Association (CCA). I don't remember how we obtained it or who gave us their information. Most likely, it was the surgeon's office.

We received CCA's newsletters in the mail every quarter. The front cover usually showcased a photo of a child with a craniofacial syndrome, along with their story. I thrived on reading others' stories, some with the same syndrome, and others with different craniofacial conditions.

On the one hand, it was nice to discover there were other people like us. I didn't feel so alone in this journey, even if we were thousands of miles apart.

On the other hand, there were the occasional articles honoring someone who had recently passed. I silently grieved as I stared at the cover photo with the words: *In memory of.* I felt fear begin oozing its way back into my mind.

Would this be us? Our son on a cover… "in memory?"

I wondered if the death of our child before adulthood was something Steve and I should be preparing for.

I felt relieved and lucky we still had our son. Was it wrong? Was it normal I was guilt stricken for feeling lucky?

There was little research on Apert Syndrome, and no valid statistics hypothesizing the life expectancy of a person born with Apert Syndrome. We had never seen anyone with this syndrome before, especially with odds of 1 in 160,000.

****

Over the next couple of years, Logan started blossoming. He was two and a half years old, running around getting into everything, and exploring his world with his new hands.

I had finished my second year of teaching special education, so I was ready to put my skills to use. During the summer, I spent time working with him on increasing his speech and improving fine motor skills. He had an abundance of developmental toys to explore using his new dexterity.

He learned to hold his sippy cup using both hands, eat finger foods, and hold a spoon. Spoons were the biggest challenge, so I bought him some baby spoons with curved handles. These were easier for him to grasp. I adored the way he would put his thumb and middle finger together even though they couldn't bend, and pick up little pieces of cereal. It reminded me of a lobster pinch. Even though he wasn't physically able to bend his fingers, he was adapting.

****

By the end of the summer, Steve had already gone back to work for football two-a-days practice. Logan and I were enjoying the last few weeks of summer before I had to return to work. I was starting a teaching position with a new school district, which also had an employee daycare on the campus where I would be working. I was comforted knowing he would be so close while I worked.

One day the doorbell rang. I opened the door and stepped outside to speak to a nice sales lady selling subscriptions to the local newspaper. I didn't typically open my door to any salespeople, but I did this time for some reason. We had a glass storm door, so I left Logan right inside playing where I could still see him. I knew if I let him outside with me in the front, he would want to take off. He loved going for walks and was definitely a busybody.

We spoke for a little bit, and it turned out she had worked in the same school district as Steve. She was selling papers on the side for extra money.

"Ok, I'll take a subscription. I like to look at the sale ads and clip coupons from the Sunday paper. Steve will want it for the sports section though," I said sheepishly. "Let me go inside and get my checkbook if you don't mind. I'll be right back," I added.

I walked inside, grabbed my checkbook, then stepped back outside and closed the glass door. After I gave her the check, she and I made small talk for a few minutes. She looked over my shoulder and asked, "Aw, is that your son?" I turned around and saw Logan standing there, peering through the glass, grinning at us.

"Yes, it is."

"How old is he?" she asked.

"He's two and a half," I replied. As soon as the words came out of my mouth, I heard, *click*. I turned back around to see Logan still standing there with a big smile on his face.

"Did he just lock the door?" the lady asked.

I pulled on the handle to try and open the door.

"Oh my gosh, he did! Shoot!" I declared.

To give you a sense of my astonishment, let me explain the structure of Logan's hands and fingers. Even though all his fingers were surgically separated, we knew he would never be able to bend and flex his fingers the way most of us do. Part of the fusion also included the joints. So, in essence, he had no knuckles, which are the joints in the bones to allow bending movement.

The lock on the glass storm door was approximately the size of a quarter. It was like a twist handle on a gumball machine, only smaller. It took a perfected pincer grasp to turn it.

The lady and I stood there for a few seconds, and then she asked, "Do you think your back door is unlocked?"

"Well, I am a creature of habit, and I was taught to always lock doors, so honestly, I doubt it will be unlocked," I replied.

"If you want, I don't mind staying right here if you want to go check. That way, I'll be right here, just in case he unlocks it and tries to open the door," she offered.

We lived on a corner lot, so our street was the main road connecting a back way out of our neighborhood. It accompanied a lot of traffic at times, so I appreciated her offering to keep watch so he didn't escape into the street.

"Oh, thank you so much. I'll be right back," I responded. I jogged along the side of our house, opened the gate, and walked into the backyard. *Please Lord let the door be unlocked.* I tried the doorknob. It was unlocked. *YES*! I sighed with relief. I went inside, picked up Logan, put him on my hip, and stepped outside.

"Thanks for waiting," I professed.

"You're welcome. You have a cutie on your hands. He's tenacious," she smiled.

"Yes, he is, thank you," I smirked.

The lady left and we went back inside.

Hmph. She didn't even flinch at his appearance. Her words were kind, too...No looks of pity. It's like we were normal people to her. I like this lady.

I giggled afterward at the irony of the situation. I had to call my sister to share with her the good news: *My kid just locked me out of the house! Can you believe it? I felt proud that he could manipulate the small door lock. My kid is pretty dang awesome. Although, I hope he doesn't make a habit of this. Good grief. What's he going to do to me when he is a teenager?*

****

Articulation is a wonderful skill

Another developmental skill he still needed to work on was his expressive language and speech articulation skills. I taught him a few hand signs for words like *more, please, thank you, all done,* and *drink.* He mastered these pretty well, then verbalized the words with the sign language.

He was receiving speech therapy through the half-day Preschool Program for Children with Disabilities (PPCD) class at the school where I worked. I felt very fortunate because this PPCD class was also an inclusion class in our employee daycare.

He then remained in the daycare room until I got off of work. Being around typically developing children helped him tremendously. He was putting words together to form short sentences, but some sounds were still difficult for him to articulate.

He also had some low tone with oral motor skills, which affect the muscles around the mouth. He drooled excessively, cultivating the need to wear a bib all day.

With his articulation, he often replaced the tr-blend with an 'f' sound. It was easier to produce since he couldn't form the proper tongue placement for consonant blends.

One day my mom and I took Logan with us while we were Christmas shopping. He was only about three, and he had begun talking in phrases.

As we strolled through the toy store, we wheeled our cart over to the aisle with all the trucks. Logan loved any kind of truck or car you could imagine. You name it, he loved it: fire truck, dump truck, eighteen-wheeler truck, monster truck, or a plain old pickup truck. He was sitting in the shopping cart while we were looking at some of the remote control cars and trucks. His eyes were as big as the moon. Anything that goes *vroom* was his eye candy. Then, he spotted it. On the top shelf, he pointed to a colossal, granddaddy of all remote control vehicles.

"Big tuck! Big tuck!" He proclaimed as if he had discovered the Rolls Royce of all trucks. Only, he didn't say tuck. It was a bit like the scene from the movie "Christmas Story." If you've seen the movie, you know the one I am talking about. The boy Ralphie had said a curse word as his dad was changing the tire on their car.

I could feel the slow motion of my head turning in his direction as the inadvertent curse word came out of his mouth. Logan's mispronunciation was unintentional, of course. I held back a gasp as the gentleman on the same aisle looked at us like a deer in headlights. Everything and everyone, including time, stood still. And before I could correct him, he said it two or three more times, as loud as he could. He was thrilled.

It was awkward, yet like a hilarious scene from a sitcom. I could almost feel the imaginary video camera zoom back and forth from my face to the other customers standing around. I looked over at my mom, and her shoulders were moving up and down, trying her best to stifle her giggle.

I said to him, "yes, yes, that is a big TRRRR-uck."

I looked to the man standing there next to us and gave him a smirk, while he still stood there staring.

After we got to the car, we were both laughing hysterically. As inappropriate as it was, and even though out of all the curse words he said probably the worst one there is, the awkward situation left me… proud. Yes, my sense of humor is a bit twisted, but darn it, I was proud my kid was starting to talk. *We just need to work on those consonant blends.*

****

About a month later, we had an annual meeting for Logan at school. The purpose of the meeting was to discuss his present levels of academic and functional skills. We also developed and discussed recommendations for a plan based on his needs over the next year. They call it an Individual Education Plan (IEP).

The speech pathologist explained TR-consonant blends may develop at a little older age. So, developmentally, he wasn't required to master those sounds for a few more years.

Needless to say, I had a special request for the speech pathologist. I told them the story of the visit to the toy store.

She politely obliged and wrote new goals to work on his articulation. We all shared a giggle about it at the meeting. The humor of it all gave me some comfort and reassurance. These meetings don't always have to be so serious.

Chapter 9
Alien Face

"Tis true my form is something odd, but
blaming me is blaming God..."

~ *Isaac Watts*

Taking Logan out into public was never a question for me, despite any fear of the stares or odd looks from others. Quite frankly, he did not look different to me. I knew the minute we brought Logan home from the hospital I would not sequester ourselves. Personal pep talks became my routine before heading out to the store or any public place. I reminded myself, people would look because they were curious. Presumably, most people had never seen anyone with this type of appearance. (i.e. bulging eyes, misshapen head, fused hands and feet). I would be curious as well. Yet, I've learned there was a window for processing these kinds of things. Humans are innately curious. Besides, I wanted to believe the world is full of good people. I was hopeful they would not discard us, but see us as human beings, living a journey like any other family.

Passion and fire burned inside of me. God did not bless us with this child to live in isolation and shame. As a matter of fact, I felt it was quite the opposite. There were things to see, feel, hear and learn. Life is full of so many great things, and I refused to let the world ostracize us and send us to an exile island.

I made trips to stores, pushing Logan around in the shopping cart while he lay in the infant carrier. People who we passed would look and do a double-take.

I expected it, so I would smile at them, hoping they would see us as real people. A few would smile back, and many would look away and keep walking. I decided I would give people the benefit of the doubt. I imagine they didn't know what to do or say and were curious. So I forgave their ignorance and kept smiling at people. Quite a daunting task at times.

To the ones who didn't return a kind gesture, my routine became habitual: Put on a fake smile. If I smile enough on the outside, maybe it will seep into my inside. Don't let them see your pain.

Rather than stare, I wish people would ask me questions…anything. Ask me how old he is, what his name is. General questions are always safe if you're uncomfortable asking about his syndrome. At least it acknowledges that you see us as worthy humans.

What I really wanted to do some days was to rip off my filter and blurt out some choice phrases: *What are you looking at? What is your problem? Can I help you with something? Do you mind not staring? Hey, how about you mind your own beeswax?* Yet, I knew that if I opened that can of worms, it would only lead down another road full of hurt. It might make me feel better for a split second, but at the end of the day, it would only make the wounds hurt more. So instead I decided to search for the ones who display warmth in their eyes… find warmth and compassion - not pity. I yearned for others to see what I saw—God's love and beauty.

Yet, there were times when fear won. Some days it was too much for my heart. I found myself weary and exhausted from the day, so I couldn't muster up the courage to deal with judgment from others. I didn't want to feel sad every time we went out in public because I observed the way people looked at my child. So, in those days, we stayed in our happy place, our home. And that was okay too.

****

One day I met up with a friend for lunch. She was a speech therapist at my previous school, and she invited me to meet her and her daughter for lunch. Her daughter was about six years old and loved meeting Logan.

We decided to go have lunch so we could sit and visit while our children played. They be-bopped around the indoor play place and crawled up and through the jungle gym.

Logan was barely big enough to play on the play place, but still small enough he needed help getting up a few climbs. Her daughter was so sweet to help him climb up to the platforms so he could get to the top and go down the slide. They had been playing for about fifteen or twenty minutes when her daughter came down. She had a distraught look on her face.

My friend asked her daughter, "What's wrong? Are you okay?"

Her daughter's reply actually took me by surprise.

"I'm sad because there was a kid who pointed at Logan and called him an alien face," she said, her face forlorn.

By the look on my friend's face, she was mortified with the other kids' response. It was an awkward moment for both of us. She looked at me, not knowing what to say.

I looked at *her*, not knowing what to say.

It was almost like she had a look of guilt on her face. It certainly wasn't her fault, but her empathy meant a lot to me.

She told her daughter, "That wasn't a very nice thing for that kid to say to Logan, was it? If you see them again, you can tell them to be nice to your friend."

She then looked at me again, with an 'I don't know what to say look' and said, "Lisa, I am so sorry that happened."

I fought hard, real hard, to hold back my tears. I put on my game face and replied, "It's okay, unfortunately, this seems to be part of the package deal." What a lie. It was not okay, and the emotional F5 tornado whirling through my mind was starting to do its damage. I felt the tears damming behind my eyes, now stinging. I fought them, not allowing the gates to open, at least not until I was in my car. I knew if I allowed myself to cry, it would be an ugly cry. I didn't want to cause a scene or attract any more unusual attention to our little party. We already received enough of that. This caused a new frustration for me. Feeling like I had to contain my emotions because of others' behaviors filled me with bitterness.

Uncomfortable situations like these were inevitable, but gosh darn it, they don't have to be! I wanted to hike up the jungle gym, drag the kid down by his ear, and give him a piece of my mind. The right thing to do would have been to find the mom and to introduce Logan to them, and explain his situation. I didn't even know which kid it was.

I just couldn't. It was too much. My emotions weren't ready for it yet.

Fortunately, Logan was at an age where he still didn't understand others' perceptions of him yet, which was a blessing. Someday though, I knew he would. But, *I* understood, and it hurt. I wanted to take the pain for him. I wanted this to not be what he has to deal with for the rest of his life. I didn't like knowing others perceived him as *different*. I didn't appreciate intolerance from others.

To me, he was, and still is, a beautiful, sweet little boy who likes to run, climb, play with monster trucks, and throw a good ol' tantrum with the best of them. I had to remind myself there *are* a lot of sweet and compassionate kids out there. I also realized kids could be plain mean little turds sometimes. It's our responsibility as parents to teach our children about empathy, compassion, and to be kind to others.

After this incident, my friend and I exchanged a much-needed hug. Her embrace alone gave me comfort. She understood. She may not have had the right words in the moment, but I knew she had my back. And it was what I needed.

GLOVES ARE COMING OFF NOW!

About six months later, my mom and I were out and about doing some shopping. We had Logan with us, so we decided to go and eat lunch so he could also play.

We all had our lunch, and then Logan was ready to kick off his shoes and go play. This was a different fast food place in town close to the mall. I was on guard, as always, anytime we went to public places. All seemed to be going well.

Suddenly, I heard a blood-curdling scream coming from a kid, and then I heard Logan's cry. I could tell they were two separate sounds. I shimmied my thirty-three-year-old body through the small spaces of the jungle gym, barely making it through. My stomach wrenched, worried about finding him injured. Logan still had many holes in his skull, so subconsciously, thoughts of sharp edges and brain injury still lingered.

My final ascent brought me to find a kid screaming at the top of his lungs about four inches from Logan's face. Logan was hysterically crying. This time, my gloves came off. Mama bear claws came out, and my teacher's voice echoed.

"HEY!" I yelled to get this kid's attention since he was screaming so loudly,

He stopped screaming, with a look of shock.

"Why are you screaming at him?" I vehemently asked in a stern voice.

He shrugged his shoulders, then with a matter-of-fact reply said, "He looks weird."

My lips pursed. *Deep breath in...out.*

"It's not nice to scream in someone's face! Would you want someone screaming in your face?"

He shook his head no.

"He doesn't look weird. This is how God made him, and he has feelings like you and me. You scared him and that was not nice at all. You need to tell him you're sorry!"

This was the only remedy that came to me at the moment, regardless of its authenticity.

"Sorry," he said, and then ran off.

Logan reached for me, so I held him for a moment.

"Do you want to keep playing?" I asked. He shook his head no.

We made our descent down through the germ-infested plastic tubes of the play place. As we came to the bottom I began scanning the play place. I prepared myself for some kind of confrontation from the kids' parents, saying I had no business reprimanding their child. But to no avail, there was no parent. I preferred to avoid confrontation at all costs, yet this time I wanted to go into the restaurant area on a manhunt. I wanted to have a serious discussion with the parents about their child's behavior.

Logan still needed my attention and comfort, so I didn't want to abandon him or drag him into any more trauma. So instead, my mom and I decided it was time to leave.

After that incident, we avoided fast food restaurants for a little while. It was just too much. If this is the way it's going to be, then I wanted to take a break from the public. I wanted to go to places where people didn't stare and give Logan a break from any more trauma.

However, our break was short-lived. Confinement wasn't a way to live. God reminded me again, He didn't create us to live in shame or fear. So, we continued to go to public places, nonetheless, my intuitive senses were hyper-aware of people and surroundings from then on.

****

About a year later, I wanted to try a new jumping gym not too far from our house. I figured this would be a different atmosphere anyway. This place had inflatable bounce houses and obstacle courses.

I took Logan up there, and let him run around and go through the bounce houses to exert all his energy. It also gave me a break to sit and decompress. He played for about thirty minutes and then ran over to the bench where I was sitting and crawled underneath. I thought he was being silly and playing around.

I peeked underneath, and with a giggle and grin, I said, "What are you doing, silly boy? Are you playing hide and seek?"

When I saw his expression, I knew something was wrong. He had a sullen look on his face like he saw a ghost and wanted to hide in the darkest corner he could find.

I got down on my knees and peeked underneath. "What's wrong?" I asked. He wouldn't speak. Finally, I said in a nurturing voice, "Come here sweetie, so I can talk to you, please."

Still, he wouldn't talk, and wouldn't budge. "Are you hurt?" I asked, getting really concerned at this point. He shook his head no.

So, I sat there on the floor, waiting and wondering what to do. I asked him a few more questions, probing, trying to figure out what was going on. Even though I had an inclination of what might have happened, I still wanted him to express himself. I sat for about ten minutes until he finally came out from under the bench.

"Did someone hurt you?" I asked.

He shook his head no. After several minutes, he finally spoke, "He say I'm monster."

Heavy sigh. Here we go again. My heart sank. I asked him if he could point out the kid to me. I finally felt like I was in a place, emotionally, where I could step up now and try to make this a teachable moment. Logan was at an age where he was beginning to notice other kids' reactions to him.

We looked around for him, but he must have left while I was trying to coax Logan out from under the bench. It was time for the conversation now since he was aware of others' treatment and perceptions of him.

"Logan," I began in a soft voice, "those kids don't know you as a person and it wasn't nice for them to be mean like that. I love you, and God loves you and made you exactly the way you are. It's okay for you to tell them it hurts your feelings when they say those things to you."

"Logan, if anyone says anything mean to you that makes you feel bad, you can speak up and tell them they're not being nice. Or, you could come to me, you don't have to hide."

We left the jumping place, but we did not let the incident keep us from going back. I'm not going to lie, my bruised spirit left a bitter taste in my mouth. Caution would now be my armor. *Is it going to be like this everywhere we go?*

We might be 1 in 160,000, but we are not only an anomalous statistic.

We are people with feelings.

We are a family who wants to live without being pointed and stared at.

We are a family who wants to be included.

We are a family who wants to feel accepted.

We are a family who wants to have fun.

After we got home, the forest of emotions cluttered my mind, making it hard to move.

I sat on my couch… indignant. *This is so unfair.*

There were only two options here—hide away…let everyone and everything strip down all esteem and confidence, preventing us from living a life God intended for us, or pick my head up, get up, wipe away my tears, get out of this funk, and press on.

I chose the latter. God put us here on this earth for a purposeful life, not so the world could shame us into despair. God's promise is faithful, and he helps us through what life throws our way (Nehemiah 9:7-38).

My new prayer—he will be able to do the same as he grows.

Chapter 10
The Elephant in the Room

"When one door of happiness closes, another opens; but often we look so long at the closed door that we do not see the one which has been opened for us."

~ Helen Keller

Marriage is hard. Parenting is *harder*. Add having a child with medical complexities and special needs into the mix, and you have yourself a hot mess.

It's not easy discussing marital difficulties. No one likes admitting they don't have it all together. I wish I could say everything was rainbows and sunshine with our marriage, but it wasn't.

Steve and I were fond of each other when we first started dating in 1999. We enjoyed going out with our friends a lot. We had a lot of fun and fell in love.

I remember when I first met Steve, I thought he was cute but he didn't say much. I still joke with him because at the time, I wasn't sure if he was being rude or not. We were introduced and he didn't even say hello or nice to meet you. He acknowledged me with eye contact, but that was it. Once it was only a couple of people around though, he was a bit more talkative. I thought, *oh, I guess he's a little shy or something.*

He asked me out on a date, which surprised me. I had figured he didn't even like me. I found out the next day after our first date when one of the coaches who was his best friend told my friend he was *smitten.* The rest is history.

****

We were not getting along very well the first year of Logan's life. We had only been married a year and a half when he was born, so we were still learning what marriage meant. Steve was coaching three sports and working seven days a week during football season. I became a football widow. During the fall I rarely saw him. I was somewhat resentful, even though I knew he was only doing his job. Still, I felt so alone and like I had so much of the responsibility of taking care of Logan on my shoulders. He wasn't exactly an *easy* baby. Not to mention he cried a lot.

We argued about finances, different parenting opinions, doctor appointments, work, intimacy, housework, and who knows... probably even the dog. All of these things definitely put a strain on our marriage.

I was also teaching at the time, in a self-contained special education classroom with children who had significant cognitive disabilities. I loved my students to the core, but it took every bit of my emotional and physical strength to get through some days.

Years of this took a toll on our marriage, and quite frankly, there were a few distinct times we almost separated. We were both constantly exhausted, on edge, arguing about anything and everything, in debt and financially strapped, and inevitably beginning to lose hope.

Both Steve and I were still paying on student loans, had bought our first house while I was pregnant, and had two car payments. My dad was very generous to have loaned us a couple thousand dollars in the first year to help us out with our financial status, but it was gone within a month, paying for hospital bills.

We had all the unexpected medical bills, and since we were both in the education field, we were paying a thousand dollars a month for the highest insurance plan because we knew we needed it for Logan.

There were some very humbling times when we scraped for money. One day we had a discussion because we needed money for a couple grocery items, formula, and diapers.

"What are we going to do? We need some milk, bread, and we're almost out of formula and diapers, and we *have* to have those," I asked.

"I don't know. I guess I could take something to the pawn shop in town and see if I could get some cash to cover us until we get paid," he concluded.

"You could take our video camera and see if they will give us anything for it," I suggested.

"Yeah, I guess I could. We probably won't get much, but it will be a little cash. I also have a gold chain necklace I've had for a long time. I'll take it too and see if they'll buy it."

Steve drove down to a pawn shop close in town and took our old video camera with his gold chain and hawked it for a little bit of cash.

We were down to nothing in our bank account, and trying to stay on top of our bills felt like we were robbing Peter to pay Paul. Another measure we took was deciding to trade in Steve's truck for a small car so the payments would be lower, but it only lasted about six months.

We still weren't making ends meet, so we returned our leased car back to the dealership and Steve's dad loaned us $1,500 to buy a 1988 manual transmission Chevrolet truck. Driving a stick shift was actually kind of fun. I hadn't driven one since I had my Ford Escort GT when I was eighteen years old.

This truck was quite a hoopty jalopy. We found a random button, when pushed, it turned on illuminating lights on the undercarriage of the truck. I was afraid the truck was going to start bouncing up and down with hydraulics and then begin playing "Low Rider. It was a very interesting ride, but at least it got us from point A to point B.

We took several measures to do what we had to do to make ends meet. I even tried to sell kitchen products for a while, but it took time and effort to host parties as well as getting others to host parties. I had to find a babysitter to make it all work, so it was more of a hassle than it was worth at the time.

At one point, Steve's mom had taken a collection from her church during Sunday school and sent us about $300. Even though we didn't ask for money, she knew we needed some help. It was such an unexpected surprise, which helped pay a few bills!

Wow, God must have known. We are so lucky.

****

Steve and I received a package in the mail, when I opened it up, it was from Steve's eighty-eight-year-old great aunt, Virginia (Ginna) Gray. She had written us a message.

"Steve and Lisa, Linda (Steve's mom) called me to inform me of your newborn baby. She said that his surgeon said he was a good eater and a fighter. I felt compelled to write a poem to both of you, as devastated parents, as though I am Logan talking to both of you."

The following poem brought me to my knees, sobbing, as if she knew exactly what we needed to hear:

I'll Drink My Milk and Fight
Written for Logan Brown

When I hear mommy crying
And see daddy by her side,
I'm sure they're really trying
To be brave-though mystified

But I know something they don't know
In time, I'm gonna be alright.
I know 'cause Father told me so.
If I drink my milk and fight.

God has prepared my special "Doc"
He's the best of his kind around.
When he's finished, I'll be in good shape.
My head may hurt but I'm not down.

This is not over, but soon will be.
I'll be home to stay, just wait and see.
So, mommy don't cry and don't be blue.
Lean on daddy, he wears a big shoe.

Daddy, don't fret about the bills.
You know my Father, beyond the hills.
He didn't make a mistake with me.
I'm gonna have scars, but so does He.

By Virginia Gray

My heart pounded as tears rolled down my face. I handed it to Steve, and watched his eyes well with water.

"Wow." He said, as he handed it back to me.

"Yeah, I know. This is so special, and powerful," I said.

I carried this divine message with me from time to time, allowing it to remind me that God *will* take care of us, no matter the outcome of our circumstances.

Chapter 11
Super Sibling, On the Way!

"You can't steal second base and keep one foot on first."
~ Frederick B. Wilcox

Heather Stark and I became friends back in 1999. We had both recently graduated from college, although I am six years older than her. I had gone *back* to school to change majors. She received her Bachelor's degree in Psychology from the University of North Texas, and I received my Bachelor's degree in Social Work from The University of Texas at Arlington in December of 1998.

We met when we were both hired on with a service called Early Childhood Intervention (ECI), which was facilitated through the state of Texas. ECI employed nurses, psychologists, social workers, speech therapists, physical therapists, and occupational therapists. The mission of ECI is to provide services and guidance for families of a child from birth to age three with developmental delays, medical diagnoses, or disabilities, to help them learn and grow.

She and I each occupied a position titled Early Intervention Specialist. In other words, we were case managers. About ninety percent of our time was spent in the client's home to provide education and therapies. The qualifying families had children who either already had a diagnosis or a suspected developmental delay.

We shared a small office for about a year in 1999, each of our desks facing the opposite walls. It was the first sign of a long-lasting friendship because we were continuously turning around talking and sharing stories. It was as if our desks faced away from each other on purpose, like in school.

Sometimes we laughed so hard together, we had tears. Other staff members would stop by our office to see what kind of fun they were missing. There is something about being able to laugh with another female friend, be silly, and have a good time. I quickly discovered we had the same slapstick sense of humor. Well, she had me at *slapstick.*

Our friendship continued, and we even both chose to pursue a teaching career. She started before me. Both of our husbands were already educators. I followed her footsteps a few months later.

I enrolled in an alternative certification program with the state education service center. It would take two years to complete, along with passing the state education certification exam to become a teacher.

I accepted my first teaching job on an emergency certification permit. It was allowed in Texas if you were currently enrolled in the teacher certification program.

The position I originally applied for was for a fourth grade classroom. However, I received a call from the principal, and she had hired someone else for the position. She informed me there was another classroom opening she thought I would be perfect for.

"It's a special education classroom and in a self-contained setting. There are about four students in this class, and you would have an aide to assist you."

I accepted the job and dove in headfirst. I worked in that district for four years, until I was ready for a change.

June 2004

The red light was blinking, indicating we had a message on our answering machine. I pushed the button.

"Hey, it's me, Heather," my friend half-whispered. "There's a special education position open at my school...and um...I'm not even sure if I am supposed to know about it yet. So, yeah, I wanted to tell you about it. And we have an employee daycare, so Logan could come with you and he would be in my class. Call this man, he is the principal, and he's super nice. Take your resume to the school and tell them you are interested in the job. Ok, so, I gotta go, I'll talk to you later." The answering machine beeped.

After listening to her message, I wrote down the number she left on the answering machine and called the principal. I attended two interviews.

A week later I received a call from the principal. "Hello Mrs. Brown, I wanted to let you know we have made our decision, and it is my pleasure to offer you the position for the self-contained PPCD classroom," he said. His voice was so cheerful, kind and sincere.

"Oh, wonderful! Thank you so much, and I accept your offer. Thanks for the call, and I am really looking forward to working with you," I replied.

I was super happy. My mom had been taking care of Logan for me while I worked, but I knew it was time to give her a break. I wanted him to start socializing around other kids, and receive his therapies through school once he turned three years old.

****

August 2004 - Time for baby talk

I'll be honest. It was a process in making the decision to have another child after experiencing medical complexities with Logan. There's a fear of it happening again.

Steve was hesitant at first about the idea of having another child, but for some reason, I was not. I knew with every ounce of my being

I was supposed to have another child. I won't lie and say I didn't have any anxieties about what could happen. Yet, I felt a deep sense of trust God would bless us with another child and everything would be okay.

I also felt if I didn't get pregnant, it was not in His plan for us, and I accepted it. I felt at peace with it, a rather buoyant attitude. But, I wanted Steve to be at peace as well.

Steve is a quiet guy, never letting anyone know when something bothers him unless it is about sports or traffic. He is very passionate about both, positively and negatively. Albeit, this ordeal we experienced created a wound...for both of us, but because he internalized everything, it took a toll on his spirit.

****

When Logan was around two, I found an opportunity to bring up the idea of having another baby...*gently*. We previously attended genetic counseling, which resulted in the explanation of odds of us having another baby with Apert Syndrome was approximately 0%. Since it was a fluke mutation, neither of us carried the gene.

Steve said no at first. He didn't want either of us to go through what we had already gone through, and I didn't either. Regardless, something told me it was going to be okay this time. So, I gave Steve a little space and didn't bring it up again for a while.

A few months passed, and I still felt the stirring inside of me to have another baby, so I brought up the issue again.

"What do you think about having another baby?" I asked apprehensively. "The geneticist said our chances of having another Apert child is 0%," I observed, as Steve processed what I presented to him. He didn't completely balk this time.

"I don't know...maybe."

That was good enough for me, so I was happy he was considering it. "What if we pray about it and leave it up to God? Whatever happens, or doesn't happen, then I will accept it as God's plan," I professed.

He quietly processed it for a few minutes. "Okay, that's fine," he said.

"Okay then. We will see what happens." I felt like I was going to explode with excitement, but contained myself.

I grew up with siblings, and even though we fought like cats and dogs at times, we are very close. Steve also grew up with a younger brother. I knew if I had another child, he or she may or may not have the same relationship as I did with my siblings. Yet, at the same time, I knew Logan would always have family, and I did worry about him being alone when he grew up. So, my prayer went like this:

"God, I would really like to have another child. I will be happy with another boy or a girl, but please bless us with another child."

Two months after I had accepted the job at the other district, I found out I was pregnant.

****

I had another great pregnancy, and at four months, we found out we were going to have another little boy. Truth be told, I looked at little girl crib bedding, just in case, but had saved all the crib bedding we used with Logan. My heart fluttered, and I was so thankful to God for blessing us with another child.

When I went in for my last prenatal visit, my doctor scheduled to induce me on Saturday since he was on call. I only had four days until my actual due date. So, Friday night we took Logan out to my parents' house for him to have a sleepover so I could prepare for induction the following morning.

As I prepared and packed my overnight bag and made sure the nursery was ready, I had some sharp pains I didn't recognize. They went away after a few moments, so I didn't think anything of it. It happened again about an hour later and then subsided. It was nothing like the pains I remembered having after they induced me with Logan, so I brushed it off.

I packed everything I needed and went to bed to try to get as much sleep as possible, even though at this point in the pregnancy, sleep was pretty much nil. I felt like I needed a crane to hoist me up and turn me over in bed. Not to mention, Mr. Heartburn and Mrs. Reflux jolted me up out of bed every night. Nonetheless, excitement and anxiety wrapped up with a nice bow on top stole my slumber. Tomorrow would be the day to open the gift.

****

Saturday, April 30, 2005

We got up bright and early and arrived at the same hospital where Logan was born, with my same doctor delivering.

The nurse began prepping my hand for the IV.

"Hmm...are you nervous?" she inquired after sticking me four times trying to find my vein.

"Not really...I don't feel like I am nervous," I responded. I told myself that morning everything was going to be okay. Perhaps the memories flooding over me subconsciously snuck up on my nerves.

The doctor came in to check my status. "Lisa, you've already dilated to three centimeters," he stated matter of fact.

Sweet! Maybe this won't take as long. It dawned on me that my labor began last night, but since I hadn't recognized the pains I experienced, I didn't even know that's what it was. This labor was completely different from Logan. It was only the early stages, so it wasn't unbearable pain.

"I'm working in my office today, so the nurse will take good care of you until it's time for delivery," he said, then he walked out of the room.

****

"Let me know when you are ready for the epidural and I can call for the anesthesiologist," the nurse said.

This time I thought, *okay, I want to give it a try and wait it out as long as I could, not asking for it too early so it didn't prolong my labor.*

I dilated to six and finally said, "Okay, I am ready for the epidural now."

The anesthesiologist showed up, and the epidural went in *successfully* with the first try.

"Okay Lisa, I am going to eat lunch, but I will be right outside your room at the nurse's station. If you start feeling a lot of pressure, call and I will come to check on you," my nurse offered.

****

Our parents left to go eat some lunch, thinking it would probably take some time before I was ready to deliver.

I turned to Steve after about thirty minutes, "Hey, I think I am feeling some real pressure down there, will you push the nurse call button?" I stated.

Steve looked at me with a sly grin, "What?" But it's only been thirty minutes since she checked you last. No way it could be time already, it's not that bad," he said half-jokingly.

I gave him a look, and with conviction in my voice I facetiously replied, "Well if you want to be the one to catch this baby in a little bit, suit yourself."

He smirked, then obliged and pushed the nurse button for me. "My wife is feeling some pressure, could you please send the nurse to check on her?" he requested.

"Yes, she will be right in," said the lady on the other end of the nurse call box.

A few minutes later the nurse walked in, "You're feeling some pressure now?" she asked.

"Yes, I know I am numb from the epidural, but I do feel like there is pressure now," I replied.

She checked me, and then exclaimed, "Well, you are fully dilated to a 10! I need to page the doctor to come in now, so do *not* push Lisa. Keep your breathing calm and try to relax until the doctor comes in."

My inner dialogue began. *Yes! This all seems so easy. Ok, don't push. Don't... Push. And... don't panic. Everything will be okay, this time. Won't it?*

As soon as the doctor came in and 'suited up' he said, "Okay Lisa, we're ready for you to push now. Take some deep breaths and push while Steve counts, and then take a break between each push."

I pushed maybe four times, and into the world our second sweet son came!

Just like that. Holy cow, what a piece of cake! Thank you Lord, for allowing this to be easy on me this time, and thank you for this child.

I then took a deep breath, and asked, "How is he doing, is he okay? He sure is quiet."

He was much quieter than Logan had been, and he wasn't screaming and crying right away. It took several seconds before I ever heard any noises.

To my relief, the doctor replied, "Yes, he is doing just fine," as he wrapped him up and laid him on my chest. I stared down at his little face, and elation filled my soul. I smelled his newborn scent and showered his face with kisses.

As I looked down at him, I whispered, "Hi there. I'm your mommy. I love you so much, and I'm so glad you are here. Your name is Landon, and you have a big brother who wants to meet you."

I'm so glad God gave you to us. I hope that you will know how much I love you, and prayed to have you. You're big brother will need a lot of attention sometimes, but please know that doesn't mean I love you any less.

Will he understand? Will he resent me? Will Logan understand our decision to have another child? Will he think we are trying to replace him? Will he be jealous of Landon? Will Landon resent Logan?

I was plagued by the uncontrolled thoughts and questions. The only way I knew how to handle this situation was to give it to God.

****

The doctor walked out into the waiting room to tell our parents that Landon had arrived.

"He's a perfectly healthy little boy. I finished up her care, so you all are welcome to go visit now."

Hunger pangs hit me like a ton of bricks. "I'm starving," I said to my nurse aide, Can I have food now?" I pleaded.

"Yes, as a matter of fact, the doctors ordered pizza for all the nurses and there's a lot left out there. Would you like me to bring you some?" she asked.

"Oh my gosh, that would be great! Is there any chance I could also get a Coke too?" I asked sheepishly. "I don't care what brand it is, pizza and a soda sound so good right now! Thank you so much!" I resounded.

The last time I gave birth, it was a dismal affair. They all walked into my room anxious to see me holding a healthy baby boy; instead I was shoving pizza in my mouth and drinking a soda.

"Wow, that was fast," one of them laughed. Everyone began passing him around. My parents had brought Logan up to see his new brother, and we were all finally together. We gave him a small gift for becoming a big brother, so he was excited to open it up. It was one of his favorite things, a small monster truck.

Steve sat on the couch and said, "Logan, come sit by me. Do you want to hold him?"

"Uh-huh," Logan replied.

They laid his little brother, all bundled up like a burrito, in his lap while Steve helped hold him. Those few minutes were plenty of big brother time for him when he was ready to play with his toy.

I stayed in the hospital until Monday, and they allowed him to stay in my room with Steve and me.

My mom brought Logan up to visit each of those days until it was time to go home. While we were packing up all of our stuff, I found a medium size baseball made from vinyl. I started looking it over and noticed there were several signatures all around it, and the first one I noticed was from the doctor. He signed his name: *The Catcher* written under his signature. We weren't even sure who had bought this baseball, but perhaps we got ourselves a little slugger.

My family was complete and my heart was full.

****

So much happened over a three year span, and I realized it was time to update family and friends again with another letter:

September 17, 2005

Dear Family and Friends,

It has been quite some time since we've written to update everyone on how Logan is doing, but like they say sometimes...no news is good news. However, we do have good news to share regarding Logan and his little brother. Yes, that's right, we have an addition to our family. We had another little precious boy on April 30, 2005. He weighed 8 lbs. 1 oz., 20 ½ inches long. His name is Landon Wesley Brown. Logan was so excited when he finally arrived and has been having fun being a big brother. He helps Mommy by putting diapers in the trash and giving Landon a bath. Landon is 4 ½ months old now and is doing great. He loves watching Logan play.

Steve is still coaching at Castleberry High School in Fort Worth, and I got a teaching job in White Settlement school district last year. I still teach the PPCD (preschool program for children with disabilities), and the great thing about my district is that they have a daycare at my campus for all district employees to bring their children. They even have an infant room for the little precious babies, so I can see my children all the time. Landon is in the infant room and Logan is in the Pre-K room (he started last year), and has made great strides. His speech has caught up to where it is suppose to be with the exception of some articulation errors in which he received speech therapy for. As far as his hands, he has adapted very well and can pretty much do what most of the other kids can do, and then some. (He runs the VCR, DVD player, Play Station...you name it, he can do it). He receives occupational therapy to help with his pre-writing skills, and also some other fine motor skills. Logan is now 3 ½ and can spell his name, sing songs, say the ABC's, color and mark with crayon, and he just came home the other day with a paper where he wrote the letter A all by himself. He can count past 20, knows all his colors and shapes...I could go on and on to brag on our little 'angel boy.'

We just went to Dallas at the end of August for his yearly check up with Dr. Salyer, and he said that we would probably have to do another cranial vault remodel before he does the mid-face surgery. We discussed timing of the next surgery, because he will most likely be able to go to regular Kindergarten. Preferably, the mid-face surgery is to be done before he starts Kindergarten because it is a longer process. We are expecting him to want to do the next cranial vault probably this time next year, or a little later. We will go back in a year and see. Until then, we keep on keepin' on. We are very thankful for two beautiful boys who are healthy and happy.

Thanks again to all who pray for us! It has made a difference in our lives!

Hope you enjoy the pictures!

Until next time,

God Bless,

Steve, Lisa, Logan & Landon Brown

Chapter 12
Time Marches On

"The hardest prison to escape is your mind."

~ *Unknown*

For the next several years, we had a good run with no surgeries or procedures, a long overdue respite. We were ready for our little boy to finally have the opportunity to *be* a little boy and start growing and learning. Steve and I were ready to be *home*-parents and not *hospital*-parents.

Cognitively, he seemed to be keeping up...learning his name, numbers, letters, walking, running, and more of those early childhood skills.

It was a joy watching him learn new things and overcome more obstacles. He worked wooden puzzles, learned to use adaptive scissors, colored with markers, put together Mr. Potato Head, and the list goes on.

I'd like to say it was smooth sailing, but other challenges arose. Logan had some sensory processing deficits. In other words, certain situations and stimuli caused him stress and overstimulation, which often led to emotional meltdowns. It was hard to understand at times, leaving Steve and me feeling helpless, not knowing what to do. The sensory processing deficit was still somewhat of a new thing, too. It was overwhelming, mostly because Logan couldn't express *how* he was feeling that triggered these meltdowns.

This took a toll on our marriage. I understood the concept of sensory integration a little more than Steve since I taught special education, but I certainly didn't know everything. Steve was more of a disciplinarian, and I was the softy, so our parenting styles clashed like titans.

I also felt deep down in my mommy's gut that Logan might have some attention span issues as well. He would run all over the place and had a difficult time sitting still. I discussed this with the pediatrician, and again her recommendation was focused on discipline.

I was disillusioned. As his mom, I knew his extra energy was not ill-intended. He was a sweet boy. He wasn't trying to be *"a bad kid,"* as society sees kids with a limited focus. Was he incorrigible at times? Yes, he was, and he still is. He is a strong-willed child. But, what I saw he needed was patience, structure, exposure, teaching, and love. I had all of them, but I didn't always have patience. My patience ran a long way...until it didn't. I felt guilty those days when I was so tired and frustrated and raised my voice to my kids.

There was one time when I called my friend. "Heather, I feel horrible, I lost my patience and screamed at my kids. All day at work I've dealt with three-year-old students crying, throwing tantrums, my own kids crying at home, Steve is always coaching, and now I'm crying. I'm a terrible mom."

"Lisa, you are a good mom. You're human, and humans have emotions of frustration and anger, even towards those we love. Sometimes we lose our patience. It's okay, give yourself some grace. Your circumstances are very stressful right now," she reassured me.

I took a deep breath. "Thank you for saying that, and letting me get it off my chest."

"Let's pick a day after work, and you bring the boys over to play with Izzy, and you go take a few hours to yourself. Go shopping, or eat somewhere, or just take a nap if you need to," she offered.

"Oh my gosh, are you sure? Thank you so much for offering. I think I may take you up on your offer!"

I took the boys over to her house after work one afternoon and drove myself to the mall. I didn't have the money to buy anything, so I walked around going store to store, browsing at fun and pretty things. I went to the food court, bought fast food and sat there, eating and watching people go by. It was a nice reprieve, simply sitting. Some of the weight pressing down hard on my shoulders lifted for a moment. No one needed me.

****

Night Terrors

As Logan grew through his toddler years, there was an unsettling feeling about his sleep patterns. He developed something called night terrors. He would wake up at least once in the night, sometimes more, crying hysterically, yet nothing seemed to soothe him. I would get up and try to pat him in his crib. I laid down with him, turned on the music. Nothing was sufficient. I would have to pick him up and hold him and rock him until he fell back to sleep.

At around age three or four, we laid his mattress on the floor so if he rolled over and fell off the bed, it wouldn't be very far for landing. We still worried about him injuring his head. He still had large holes in his skull, so any head injuries concerned me.

He was at the age where he still needed an afternoon nap. For some reason, it was inevitable he would wake up from his nap crying and alarmingly inconsolable. I didn't understand why he was so upset after a nap when usually, kids feel refreshed, re-energized, and ready to make another disaster of the house. At least that's how I thought kids should feel after sleeping.

One night he woke up crying hysterically. He was sitting up, squirming around like he wanted to crawl out of his skin, completely incoherent of his surroundings. I tried to talk to him, but it was like he didn't even hear me, or even know I was there. He finally calmed down, and I laid down with him until he fell back asleep. I was alarmed at what I witnessed, so I mentioned this episode to his pediatrician at his next appointment.

"These are called night terrors. There is really nothing you can do about them. He will eventually grow out of them," her tone flat.

Again, I was faced with an unknown situation in which I had no control over and no solution. I didn't understand. How do they not know what causes these or what to do about them?

This continued until he was about six or seven years old. He did not sleep through the night until the age of seven. I still got up through the night, even though there wasn't anything I could do. His blood curdling scream was enough for me to at least check on him each time. What if the one time I didn't check on him was the time he was in real pain, or having intracranial pressure we were instructed to monitor?

I spent countless nights sitting beside him until he calmed down enough to go back to sleep. I spent endless hours sitting on the hallway floor outside of his room, crying and praying.

He had several sleep studies at the request of his craniofacial surgeon, to test for sleep apnea. I secretly hoped he would have a night terror during one of the sleep studies, to glean some insight from sleep technicians. I wanted them to tell me what this was, and what we could do about it. I still wasn't accepting the answers from the pediatrician, despite the information she presented to me on how common night terrors were in children under the age of six.

We checked into the hospital for an overnight sleep study one evening. The technician hooked him up to about a hundred wires, along with belts and oxygen tubes. There were night cameras mounted to the wall, a twin bed for Logan, and a recliner for me.

During the middle of the night, it happened. We always called it an *episode*, and he started screaming, squirming, thrashing around and crying.

The sleep technician came into the room, "Do you need some help?" he asked.

I was already awake, next to Logan's bedside, while he was squirming and screaming about. "Yes, please. He does this every night and after his naps," I stated with frustration in my voice.

"If he fully awakens, go ahead and unplug him and I'll take him to the restroom," I stated. Logan finally became alert, and since he was already sitting up, the technician began unhooking the leads.

"Boy, he is anxious about something, huh?" the technician asked.

His comment did not bode well for the moment. Just keep the lid on your gasket, Lisa. Up to this point, my helplessness feared there was no solution to these night terrors. Seeing them night after night, was terrifying and exhausting.

My grace was right on the ledge, ready to spread its wings and fly right out the window from his obtuse comment. With the words, *"ya think?"* sitting right on my tongue ready to project, I chose instead to let out a heavy sigh.

After the technician unhooked everything, I took Logan to the restroom and came back to the room. Within a matter of minutes, he was all hooked up again and back to bed.

A handful of hours later, the technician turned the lights on and came over the microphone in the room.

"Good morning, I will be in shortly to detach and start removing all the wires and leads," he said.

After our "no sleep," study, I wondered, *how in the world can they expect people to sleep during these, much less get an accurate analysis?*

Logan and I stirred around as the technician came in and began unplugging everything for the final time. The number of stickers for the electrical probes, belts, plugs, and buttons all hooked to one little person was astonishing. He looked like a mad scientist trying to call the mother ship home. To make it fun, I think they should play the theme to Close Encounters of the Third Kind at the end of the sleep study.

Once everything was removed, the fun part was trying to get all the putty-like glue out of his hair. It was hardly a joyful time. Not only was he starving this early in the morning, but also I had to put him in the shower, which he already hated.

The glue was cemented to his scalp, but I had to at least try to get a little bit of it out so it wouldn't be stuck for days. I knew he wouldn't be able to eat breakfast until later since he was scheduled to have an MRI first thing that morning under sedation.

I prayed for patience through the whole trauma of it all. After a few attempts at removing the glue in his hair, I finally decided it wasn't worth the fight. It was almost as tortuous as them sticking him with an I.V.

I helped him get dressed then we trucked back to the radiology floor. He was put under sedation to remain completely still for the MRI.

Twenty minutes later, the anesthesiologist carried him out to me in a warm blanket. We left to go straight to the cafeteria to get breakfast.

We got the results back several weeks later, resulting in mild sleep apnea. The only recommendation made was for us to keep a watch on him until time for him to have another surgery to advance his midfacial bones.

I thought we were already keeping an eye on him. So nothing's changed. Gotta keep on keeping on. What else is there to do?

No CPAP was recommended for his apnea, and he still had room for brain growth, thank goodness. The only thing we were left with was befuddlement.

I struggled with *no answers.* So, I searched on the Internet for night terrors in children. The limited information I found validated children who had night terrors would, in fact, *grow out of them.* I was forced to accept what I did not understand.

Chapter 13
Change Is A-Comin'

"Life is change, growth is optional. Choose wisely."

~ Unknown

August 2006

There's truth in the fact that teachers' salaries are not lofty, so making ends meet was difficult, especially with the medical bills.

We were fortunate to have health insurance, but the cost was killing us. However, choosing the highest coverage also meant it was the highest cost. Steve coached three sports for a small stipend, which took up about ninety percent of his time during the week and on weekends.

It felt like we were treading water financially. Not only working so many hours to pay all the bills but to stay afloat. Even though we had decent insurance, in addition to the premiums, we still had medical bills coming in, and Logan didn't qualify for Medicaid.

****

Steve spoke to a former student he coached who had recently graduated, wanting to know what he was doing now. He was a good kid, and his girlfriend was also a student whom Steve had coached in softball. We used her as a babysitter from time to time. She was the only one outside of the family who we trusted to watch over Logan the few times Steve and I wanted to go out to dinner.

"Um...I talked to this kid I coached who graduated last year. He got a job working for the railroad and makes good money. He also said their health insurance is great," Steve explained.

He proposed a complete career change. I sat, staring at him like a deer in headlights and processed this for a moment.

"So, what exactly would you do?" I asked.

"Well, I have to start out on the trains, then maybe I can work my way up in the future," he replied. "Basically, this would get my foot in the door."

"You will actually be *driving* trains?" I responded. What seemed like a hundred questions flooded my brain. "Are you going to have to travel? If you do travel, will you be leaving us for a long period at a time? How long will you be gone? What about living expenses for you? How is this going to work?" My interrogation didn't give him enough time to answer the first question before moving on to the next.

He looked at me as if to say*: Are you finished asking questions yet?* but instead said, "Well, let me explain first. I will start out as a conductor first. They will pay me during training, but it won't be the same salary as when I actually become a conductor. The requirement is that I am on call twenty-four hours a day. The kicker is I will be going to Wyoming for several months during training," he finished.

"Wyoming?" I half-shouted.

"Yes, Wyoming. But, the good thing is that your sister and her family live in Wyoming, so at least I'll have our family near. The bad thing is that my training will be in a tiny town called Greybull, which is about a three-hour drive from where Lori and Scott live. I'll have to rent a place, but there are a few other guys having to do the same. We talked about sharing a place to rent to cut down on the costs," he sputtered all in one breath.

****

I processed it for a few days. We discussed it a bit more, and we both agreed this was what was best.

Steve is not one to make impulsive decisions or many decisions at all. He is a processor. I knew by the conviction in his voice and words, God must have directed him on this one.

I was comforted knowing my sister and her family lived in Wyoming. They wouldn't be in the same town, but at least they were a few hours away in case he needed help.

He was to go through Conductor school, and once he completed his training, he would be 'on-call' 24 hours a day. Once he was a Conductor for a certain period, he would then be able to train as an Engineer.

Steve's goal was to be hired by the railroad company and earn more money and better health insurance. It was a tough decision because he loved sports, so it was a complete career change. But, family needs came first. Ultimately, he hoped to get his foot in the door long enough to move up into the headquarters office located near us in Fort Worth, Texas, where he would be back home.

"Are you absolutely sure you want to do this?" I asked. "Sports are your world and coaching is the closest thing you have to it."

"Yes, sports *are* my world. That's all I wanted when I was in high school. My ambition was to play professional baseball once I graduated. I was even offered a small baseball scholarship to a community college. I didn't accept the scholarship for various reasons, mainly listening to what other kids had to say about the college and coach instead of making my own decision…and I regret it. I would give up my left arm to play baseball. But, this is what I have to do. It's the best thing right now for our family."

****

"Daddy is going to be working on the choo-choo trains," I explained to our boys with as much excitement I could assemble. Fear of the unknown stared me in the face. The thought of becoming a working, single parent (by proxy) of a fifteen-month-old, and a four-year-old wasn't appealing.

I worried once he left and got away from all the stress of raising two young kids, one with complex medical needs, he might get a little too comfortable and not want to return. *What if he doesn't want to come back? What if we grow apart? All of the what if's...just what my brain needs.*

I mentally prepared by offering myself a pep talk. *Toughen up. Be strong for your kids. God will get us through this somehow.*

Yet, my questions perpetuated. *How are we going to pay for this house, my car payment, our bills, his rental living situation, his bills, and living expenses? Lord, help us.*

Knowing it would only be a temporary move for him is what gave me peace of mind. So, I shifted my mindset and supported his decision.

We can do this.

Farewell for Now...Goodbyes Suck

August 2006, at around 6:30 a.m., Steve packed up all he needed and loaded it into the car. The day he left was also the day I had to start back to school for teacher in-service. We had flip cell phones, so there was no texting. The boys and I were ready for school.

Steve hugged and kissed them and told them he would send some postcards and pictures of trains.

I turned on some cartoons for the boys, and walked out into the garage with Steve.

I handed Steve a 4 x 6 photo album I had put together for him with a bunch of pictures of the boys, our dog, and our wedding photo.

"All right, I love you," I said. "Keep this and look through it from time to time, so you don't feel lonesome.

"I love you too," he replied.

"Be extra careful on your drive. Call me as soon as you make it to Raton, New Mexico," I pleaded.

We made this trip in the past since my sister lived in Wyoming. Our route consisted of driving through Amarillo, Texas and up through the panhandle. The halfway point was in Raton, New Mexico, where we stopped to stay in a hotel right between the mountains.

"Okay, I will. I'm not in a hurry, so I'll be fine," he replied.

We hugged, but I made him hug me longer than he preferred. Steve is not a *touchy-feely* kind of person, but I'm a hugger.

"Everything is going to be okay. It'll all work out," he whispered in my ear.

"Okay, I know, somehow it will," my voice managed to utter with quivering lips.

Steve got in the car, started the engine, and drove away.

I waved as I watched the car pull away from our house. I waited to go inside until he turned the corner at the end of the street, where I could no longer see him.

My body felt like lead. The Texas humidity in August made it even harder for me to breathe. Beads of sweat ran down my back making my shirt stick to my body.

I walked into the house and checked on the boys who were still watching cartoons. I traipsed down the hallway, went into the bathroom, and closed the door. I sat on the lid of the toilet and sobbed.

A couple minutes later, I heard the twist of the doorknob. The voice of my four-year-old jolted me back to reality. He still wasn't able to turn round doorknobs, so his voice spoke through the crack of the door.

"Mommy, you goin' potty?" Logan asked with his sweet voice. I breathed in through my nose and exhaled out of my mouth. I then wiped my face with my hands and cleared my throat.

"I'm almost finished, sweetie. I'll be there in a minute," I replied. His little footsteps pitter-pattered off. I brushed my teeth again, touched up my make-up, and stared at myself in the mirror. "I can do this...I *can* do this," I whispered out loud.

I opened the door, walked down the hall to the living room. "Okay, kiddos, time for school!" I exclaimed with a cheerful tone.

I loaded up the boys in the car, and off to school/work we went. My thoughts began coaching me, *"this is not forever...stay strong...there are a lot of people depending on you to keep it all together.*

My husband depended on me…my boys needed me...my students with special needs along with their parents counted on me...and my principal relied on me. My job was to lead my classroom with a nurturing environment by helping kids learn to their fullest potential every day. The weight on my shoulders became heavier every minute.

So, we carried on with life, separately. We lived frugally, to say the least. I felt comforted since my district's employee childcare happened to be on my campus. Not only that, but I moved from a self-contained PPCD class to the inclusion PPCD class. Fortunately, I was the teacher while Logan was in the four-year-old PPCD class, so I was able to see both of my boys throughout the day.

They say a teacher should never teach the same age level as their own children. I understand it now. Yet, somehow I knew I was right where I was supposed to be for our family.

So, I worked hard as a teacher and as a mother. Inevitably, I failed at both sometimes. The boys and I visited my parents quite often, and there were a few times I drove up to Steve's parents. They came down occasionally to stay a weekend with me as well. We were fortunate to have family close enough to spend time with.

****

When Steve arrived in Wyoming, he sent both boys each a post card with a message.

A couple months later, we received a letter from Steve that wrote:

08/24/06
Mommy, Logan & Landon,
I really miss you all a lot and hope I get a chance to see you at Thanksgiving or Christmas. I have been very busy with my train classes and learning how to drive a train. I worked outside the other day and learned how to connect and unhook the train cars, how to give hand signals, lantern signals, and

talk on my radio. We learned how to connect the air hoses and put in a new coupling of the brake. I took a really long test today and got 94 out of 100 correct. I have another 60 question test tomorrow.

I'm sending some pictures I took on my way here, of my hotel, of some trains, and some antelope at Aunt Lori's house. There are some really big mountains up here that are in the pictures, and a lake next to a snow ski resort. It is a small ski slope, but you can see the trails between the trees.

Logan, give Mommy and Landon a big hug and kiss for me, and Mommy give Logan and Landon a hug and kiss. Be good and listen to Mommy's words and be her big helper. I love you guys and miss you a bunch. Hope to see you soon.

Love,
Daddy

About three weeks later, we received our second letter from Steve:

09/13/06

Mommy, Logan & Landon,

Here are some more pictures of Wyoming and the big city of Greybull. There are some pictures of the trains I have been riding on, some of my trailer that I am staying in, and the mountains.

I hope you guys are doing good and learning a lot at school. I have ten more weeks of school before I take my test to become a conductor.

Logan give Mommy and Landon a big hug and a kiss for me, and Mommy give Logan and Landon a hug and a kiss.

I miss you guys very much and look forward to seeing you soon. I love you all very much and will send some more pictures when I get another roll developed.

Love,
Daddy

Steve and I also wrote a few personal letters just to each other. I printed more pictures, and the boys colored some pictures for him. I collected everything, added some snacks, packaged it in a box, and mailed it to him.

November - December 2006

Three months had gone by. We had the entire week off from school for Thanksgiving break. I decided it was time for us to get back together as a family, so it was off to Wyoming with my boys.

Thankfully, my mom came with us on this trip. After two days on the road, we made it up to my sister's house. My brother met us there later in the week with his kids, and my dad flew up to stay for the week. It was going to be our first Thanksgiving in Wyoming.

The kids loved playing with their cousins every day, and I soaked up every moment I spent with my sister.

Steve was finishing his conducting school in Greybul, which was about three hours away. The next day he drove to my sister's house to have Thanksgiving with all of the family.

It felt good to be back together as a family. The boys wrestled around with Steve on the floor, we ate tons of food and relished in our short time together. The day after Thanksgiving, Steve was back on the road to the mountains, which meant another goodbye. The boys and I hugged and kissed him goodbye, but this time it didn't feel as difficult. Since the boys were so young, the concept of time wasn't as apparent to them as it was to me. Thankfully, I had a little more peace this time.

Steve stayed in an apartment with a few other guys who were also enrolled in the training classes. This helped somewhat with the cost of his expenses.

Once he completed the courses and passed the exams, he was certified as a train conductor. He was low on the totem pole in tenure, so the requirement was for him to work what they called the *extra board.* This meant he was on call twenty-four hours a day to relieve conductor crews who had reached their maximum hours they were allowed to work until they had to be on *a rest period.*

Railroad safety regulations did not allow conductors and engineers to have cell phones on while they worked. The only time Steve and I were able to communicate was through texting, which was a very new concept to us. We didn't text as much as we needed to because each text cost money, and we had flip phones using T9 texting. Not optimal for typing.

So, we wrote old fashioned, *handwritten* letters. This kept my spirit alive. I looked forward to getting a letter in the mail, and it was almost like a young, new romance. We stuck to this regimen over the next thirteen months. Whatever it took, I devoted myself to making this t*emporary-long distance-'single momming it' situation* work.

****

This was the first Christmas we didn't spend together. However, my sister and her family came down to Texas that year, and my brother and his family were here as well.

Unfortunately, Steve was not able to come since he was new and had no vacation time accrued. He also was considered an hourly employee, so if he didn't work, he didn't get paid.

My in-laws came down to stay with the boys so I could do some Christmas shopping. I was so grateful for them.

The holidays were challenging for me that year because all three of us were sick with strep and upper respiratory infections. *If we can just make it through this sickness running rampant through our house, then we'll be okay.*

2007

A year passed. We saw Steve only once in about every four to six months. In the meantime, I tried to keep the boys and myself busy and active. We went on walks, stroller and tricycle rides around the neighborhood, and visits to the park to play on the playground. Fast food restaurants became our place for play dates with a friend, and the jumping house was our sensory outlet. Luckily, we also had a community pool. I tried my best to keep the boys, and myself, busy and active.

There were a few times I loaded up the boys in the car to take a drive, not exactly having a destination. I took country roads all around the small town I grew up in, dreaming of moving back to the countryside someday. I wanted a yard the boys could play in and get dirty, shoot BB guns, and go on treasure hunts. My drives were perfect opportunities to reminisce about those treasure hunts.

My family did a lot of outdoor activities. We took many camping trips when I was growing up. My dad worked two, sometimes three jobs to support our family. Then the day came when he bought a camper. It felt like the most exciting thing in the world. My sister and I played in the camper even while it stayed parked in our driveway. We were excited when my dad would call my mom from work on a Friday and say, "pack the camper, we are going to the lake this weekend." Lori and I shrieked with excitement and packed as many Barbies with Barbie clothes and board games we could fit.

While we camped, my mom would take us for walks on trails sometimes. I grumbled a time or two and whined if it was really hot outside. As soon as she said, "let's go hunt for some treasure," I was all in. We found the best treasures…odd-shaped rocks, bottle caps, flowers, and fishing bobbers. You name it, we found it.

I hoped one day we could move out to the countryside where I could have some treasure hunts with my boys too. I wanted them to explore, play in the dirt, ride bikes and do fun stuff outside. We did as much as we could around our little neighborhood, but I missed the country.

****

In 2007, my parents got adventurous and made the decision to sell their house. They packed up everything and moved up to Wyoming! They wanted to explore the snowy side of the states and live closer to my sister and her family for awhile. Steve and I had also made the decision to put our house on the market with plans to move up there as well. So, more change was on the horizon. They stayed the night with the boys and me on their last night in Texas, with plans to get up early and get a head start on the road. I knew it would be a tough departure.

We had our goodbyes, and Mom and I fought tears as we hugged.

"The boys and I will be up there in a matter of months, so this isn't goodbye forever," I said. Then, they were gone.

It was fall, so school was in session again. I dropped Landon off at the one-year-old room, then walked over to the four-year-old PPCD room, where Logan would start his day of preschool.

My teaching day was split, where I was the teacher in the three-year-old room for the morning session, and the four-year-old room in the afternoon. It had already been a rough morning for Logan. He didn't want to go to school, but I got him there. Then, he didn't want to go to his class. He started crying, and pressing his feet into the ground, resisting the entrance with all his might.

I crouched down and tried talking with him to coax him into walking into the classroom. His teacher stood by the door, noticed what was happening, and walked over to help.

"Hi Logan, come on in. We've got Playdough out this morning."

Oh, I understand how you're feeling, son. I want to dig my heels into the floor too. I wish we could turn around, go back home, get back in our pajamas, and eat ice cream.

But, I knew what I had to do. With a kiss on his head, I said, "I love you, have a good day." I walked out of the door to the hallway leading to my small planning office.

The director of the daycare, who was also my friend Heather's mom, happened to be coming out of one of the other rooms directly across at the same exact time. She turned the corner to walk down the hall and took one look at me. She put her arm around me, and we walked side by side down the hallway. I was already sobbing by the time I felt her arm slide around my shoulder.

No words, and no questions. The way we met up at the same time, shoulder to shoulder, was a perfect cadence. She followed me into my little *closet* of an office that housed a desk, my computer, and craft supplies.

I sat down on my chair while she closed the door. Through my tears, I explained everything that was going on. Then, she hugged me and said with validation, "Lisa, you have great fortitude."

Fortitude. So that's what they call it? I felt more like a total train wreck.

I wanted everything to be okay, and I wanted this temporary "life change" to hurry up and be over. I didn't want to be strong anymore and do this by myself. I didn't want to hold everything together. I didn't want to feel alone.

Resentment began chiseling at my soul. *Deep down, I know why he had to leave, yet my brain still asked...why did he have to leave me here alone to deal with all of this on my own. Shouldering all the responsibility of keeping the household, raising the kids, paying the bills, and teaching children with special needs was enough to take me off in a straight jacket.* I was ready for him to come back home, and for all of this long distance lifestyle to be over. The boys started acting out more. They would argue over toys, or pretty much anything. One day I walked into the living room from the kitchen where I found both boys were coloring all over the wall. They looked at me and said, "look at what we did."

"What in the world?"

Sigh, *oh good grief.* I had to breathe deeply, and count to twenty.

I see you drew some pictures, but we don't draw or color on walls. Don't do that again. We have plenty of paper for that."

I walked into the kitchen, got two wet rags and gave them to the boys.

"Here is a wash rag, now you need to start cleaning it off."

"Okay, Mommy."

I grabbed my camera and snapped their picture, because I knew this was a moment to look back on.

I ended up cleaning most of it off, but I must say, they did a pretty good job at trying to get it cleaned off.

The boys are cleaning up crayon from the wall!

We have got to get out of the house more often.

****

On payday, we went out to eat. This is where I took them to burn off energy to a play place after their meal.

We often played outside on warm evenings in the water sprinkler or going for walks. Our backyard was approximately 30 feet by 25 feet, small and square. When it was time to come inside, it was straight to the bathtub, one boy at a time. Afterward, we read books and I tucked them in. Then, I re-tucked them in after they got out of bed numerous times.

After the boys were finally asleep, I tried to watch some TV and decompress. Inevitably, I woke up around four in the morning, still on the couch, still in my clothes. After walking my zombie-like body to bed, my alarm would wake me an hour later, just in time to get up and start it all over again.

My routine was a well-oiled machine. I needed as much structure and consistency as the boys did, if not more than they did, for my sanity.

My goal was to love my children, and most importantly, keep them alive. So I fed my kids chicken nuggets, fish sticks, or hotdogs with a veggie thrown in. When I cooked, it was a lot of Hamburger Helper, mac and cheese, and spaghetti. I felt like a crappy mom sometimes but repeated my mantra.

Just keep moving forward. Stay strong for Logan, Landon, and Steve. And by all means, for your own sanity!

I wondered if anyone else felt this way. Some days, I felt like I was losing my ever-loving mind. I longed to feel understood. I compared myself to other moms and their parenting skills. Not a choice I would make again.

****

Steve had spent the first five months as a conductor, which was basically the engineer's assistant. Conductors were the ones who got out and checked to make sure the train was built correctly. They also needed authority from the dispatchers to move, line any switches needed for the route, and do any line work to set out or pick up train cars.

He finally put in enough time and experience, so he applied to get into engineer training, which meant he would be driving the trains. He was accepted into the program and was sent to Kansas City, Kansas for the first three weeks of the program. Following those nine months of Steve as a conductor and informing me of the engineering school, I packed the car with a bag loaded with snacks for the boys. I was ready for another visit at my sister's house to reunite with Steve for a couple of days.

Before I left town, I approached my principal and told him I was resigning as a teacher.

"Mrs. Brown, are you completely certain?" my principal asked.

"Yes, I am. I have given a lot of thought to it, and we are putting our house up for sale and potentially going to move to Wyoming. If we get a contract, I need to be able to pack up and leave. I feel this would be in the best interest of the students, and my family if it happens." I replied.

I planned my route, and figured I could drive north to Kansas, stay with his aunt and uncle who still lived there, spend a few days with Steve, then drive straight west through Nebraska and South Dakota to Wyoming and stay with Lori.

My mother-in-law offered to ride with me since we would be staying with her sister, and she would fly back to Texas, while I drove the boys and me to Lori's house. My plan was not only to spend time with my sister, but also visit my mom and dad since they had recently moved up to Sheridan, Wyoming, which was about an hour away from Lori's house.

****

During our visit, Steve and I took one night for ourselves and went to a baseball game to watch the Kansas City Royals play against the Texas Rangers. It was great since we were both Rangers' fans, but Steve loves the Royals. They were his second love since he lived in Kansas for a while as a kid. Since it was the fourth of July, we had a bonus of the fireworks after the game.

The next day we spent the entire day at Worlds of Fun, a roller coaster amusement park that was also connected to a water part. We were there from open to close, trying to keep up with boys. It was a long, fun-filled, exhausting day, but they had a blast.

I chased Landon around in the small kid splash zone at the water park while Steve watched Logan go down an alligator water slide over and over.

We finally made it back over to where Steve and Logan were, and Steve looked at me with a smirk and said, "you'll never believe what just happened."

"Oh no, what happened?" I asked, my thoughts already imagining the worst.

"Logan came down the slide and told me there was a kid who kept pointing at him and laughing, telling him he looked weird," Steve explained.

"What did you tell him?" I asked with a sigh.

"Well, I told him it is perfectly okay for him to take up for himself if that kid does it again."

"Did the kid do it again?" I asked again

"Yep. Logan came up to me and said, Daddy, I did it. That boy pointed and laughed at me again, so I took his nose and did this…

and he made a pinch and twisting motion with his fingers!" Steve's smirk returned.

"Wow, he actually did that?"

"Yep. He said the kid ran off crying." Steve was now giggling.

"Hmph. Well, good for him." I could feel my chest want to bow up with pride. Not that I condone physical altercations, but dang, I was proud of him for taking up for himself.

We dried off and put our wet clothes in a locker so we could spend the rest of the afternoon riding all the rides. It was nice because this theme park had an area called Snoopy Land with tons of little kid rides. We left at dark and drove back to Steve's aunt's house and put the kids and ourselves to bed. We were so tired from all the fun from the day's events.

I laid my head on his chest as we lay there, discussing what was next when Steve completed his engineering training. He was leaving the next day, and I knew I wouldn't see him again for about six months. I tried to stay quiet, buy my tears pooled onto his chest. There really wasn't more we could say.

The next morning, Steve left to go back into town for classes. The boys and I left to drive to my sister's to stay for the week since my mother-in-law was staying a little longer with her sister and was flying back home to Texas.

****

Life was breathed back into me during our full week visit. Being back together with my sister and parents lifted some weight from my shoulders. It was time to return home from our summer trip. The boys would be starting school soon, but I was nervous about school registration, because the house hadn't sold yet. I didn't want Logan to go to the school district we currently resided in. I called Heather who had gotten me the job with the district I had just left, to see if she knew of any openings. She now worked at the brand new fine arts campus our district opened, but I knew they already filled my previous position. I had no job, and we still hadn't sold the house.

They were having Kindergarten registration that day. She told me there were a few openings left, so I went up to the school and signed him up. I also mentioned to her I was going to have to look for a new job within the district so Logan could attend.

"The employee daycare still needs a few workers," she explained.

I called the director right away and told her I was interested in working in the daycare. I was desperate. It was comforting to me also, knowing Landon would also be in the employee daycare in the room next to mine.

"Lisa, are you sure you want the teacher's aide position? You are over-qualified, and the pay isn't great. I definitely have a spot for you in the daycare."

"I am absolutely certain," I replied without hesitation.

Most importantly, I wanted Logan to continue in the same district I had taught in, where everyone knew who he was. Kindergarten is such a pivotal year for children. Kids begin noticing differences at this age but are still young and innocent enough to accept Logan for who he was, and not for any physical differences.

I knew Landon was going to do great in daycare. He was such a "go-getter." I had no doubt in my mind about what I was supposed to do. I knew it was what was best for my children.

A few people asked if I felt embarrassed for taking a demotion, so to speak, or because I went *backward* in my career. Why would I work in a daycare as an assistant with minimal pay, rather than look for another teaching position?

I was perplexed by their offensive questions. Did I have to lay aside pride since I wasn't going to be working in a position showcasing my scholarly accolades? Yes. Did I have to take a large pay cut? Yes. Without a doubt, this was something I had to do. So, why on earth would I be embarrassed about doing something in the best interest of my children and family?

Furthermore, wouldn't it degrade the wonderful employees who do this as their career? They love, nurture, and teach our very own babies while we carry on our profession.

Sometimes doing something that may seem like you're moving in the wrong direction is merely a stepping stone in another direction, which will eventually lead you to where you are supposed to be.

Was it hard? A resounding yes, because working with very young ones while you *have* very young ones at home is exhausting. But I learned so much from the ladies I worked with, and the babies I took care of.

I don't regret one single day of it. I got to know the ladies who work hard at loving our children, feeding them, and keeping them safe. Besides, I didn't have to make lesson plans, which was an enormous burden lifted. My only responsibility when I got home was to be the boys' mom, not teacher making plans and preparing for school the next day. Teacher conference periods didn't exist anymore, at least for the purpose they're called. They are used for ARD meetings, 504 meetings, RTI meetings, professional development... all educator lingo.

The trade-off of not teaching gave me more mental capacity to play with the boys when we got home. We played outside almost every day, either running through the sprinkler, going for walks around our block, or sometimes going up to the elementary school playground. It was a win-win for the three of us. This year was not going to slide through without presenting more challenges. Chaos was on the horizon. But then again, which year hasn't been chaotic so far?

Here We Go Again

Steve finished his train engineer coursework at the college in Kansas and went back to Wyoming to work as an engineer for six months. December rolled around, and I became desperate again. I drove back to Wyoming, but this time it was solely the boys and me. I packed all of the presents and put them in a huge plastic container so the boys wouldn't see. We wrote a letter telling Santa where we would be for Christmas and asked him to kindly drop off our delivery there.

A few days before we planned to head back home, Steve surprised me with another "change of plans."

"Well, there's another training class opening in January for a train dispatcher position at their main hub in Fort Worth, Texas. I went ahead and applied to see if I would get accepted into this class. I'll know in a couple of days whether or not I'm accepted," he bluntly explained, totally out of the blue.

"So, this means you might be coming home?" I asked, trying not to get my hopes up too soon.

"Yes."

The news came a couple days later.

"Um, I got accepted into the dispatching class."

My stomach flipped. I felt my shoulders relax. Lord, thank you, even though I didn't specifically ask for him to come home, You knew what we needed.

In *my* mind, he "put in his time," and so did we. He got his foot in the door like he wanted, and now it was time to reunite.

He continued, "Dispatchers have a union, and the insurance is great from what I hear."

Another hallelujah...prayers answered. We realized moving to Wyoming was not in the plan for us.

****

2008

Life was demanding once we were all back home together. We endured an adjustment period once the *honeymoon* phase was over. I tried preparing myself because I knew it was inevitable.

After all, Steve had been living without us for a year and a half. He hadn't lived the everyday needs and schedules of children. We hadn't lived with stricter rules of being quiet during the day when Dad had to work nights. So, he had to get used to living with us again, and we had to get used to living with him again.

This was also a time when Logan was really struggling in school with focusing and being still. Nonetheless, we persevered.

****

I made a decision for more change. After much discussion with Steve, I felt perhaps it was time for me to step out of the classroom and become an educational diagnostician. So, like the *pie in the sky* person I am, I enrolled in a graduate program and began working on my master's degree. It was an online master's degree program, so I figured I could handle it now that Steve was back home. This would still allow me to help in the special education program.

We decided to keep the house on the market so we could move somewhere with a bigger backyard and the boys would have more space to play outside. We had a few showings, but no offers.

Nothing was happening, so we changed real estate agents. Steve said a guy at work gave him a realtor recommendation, so we met with him. He gave us some advice to make a few updates to our house since we had lived there for seven years. So, we removed the house from the market temporarily. Steve did most of the updates himself, with the help of his and my dad for a few projects. When all the projects were completed, we put the house back on the market. Here we go again.

****

Summer came, and my parents informed us they sold their house in Wyoming and were coming back to Texas. They stayed with us for about three or four weeks while they searched for a home. They found one and moved right in at the end of summer.

Logan was starting first grade, and Landon was enrolled at my employee daycare. All was going well.

Funny how we thought we would be moving and starting a new life in another state. Things didn't really follow the plan of exactly how we had it mapped out, but we were starting to get used to this now. Learning how to let go of what we thought *should be,* and accepting how it *is,* with a go-with-the-flow mindset, relieves some of the anxiety. Steve *did* get hired to work with the railroad company as he planned, and *yes*, his benefits eventually kicked in. Yet, nothing happened in the way or order we thought it would. We understood, this was what was *best* for our family.

God had a plan for us, and moving to another state wasn't in it. Our house was on the market for a year and a half with over 50 showings, all remarking we had a lovely house, but it wasn't right for their family.

Maybe God needed us to stay in Texas.

Chapter 14
Bittersweet Halloween

"I wish everyday could be Halloween. We could all wear masks all the time. Then we could walk around and get to know each other before we got to see what we looked like under the masks."
~ *Auggie from "Wonder," by R.J. Palacio*

October came around, and it was time for Logan's annual check-up with the surgeon.

"It's time to give his brain more room and do another cranial vault," Dr. Fearon recommended. He continued, "His head circumference hasn't changed, and his skull is growing upward and his forehead is flat. He's grown significantly, so he still needs more room for brain growth. We will need to do an anterior CVR to pull the forehead out, and this should give him plenty of room for a while."

We knew he would need another one, yet we were never really prepared for it to come so quickly. It had been seven years since his last surgery, so it was a good run. We knew what to expect. This made it both easier and harder *because* we *knew* what to expect.

In the fall of 2008, we remodeled a few rooms in our home, as instructed by our *new* realtor, so we could put our house back on the market. We wanted to get a home with a little bit of land since the boys were at a perfect age to run around outside, play, ride bikes, enjoy nature, and be kids. The market had begun to dust itself off and started ascending back into the economy. We had a few looks, but not like we had expected, especially since we had updated the house.

We temporarily removed our house from the market, at least until after Logan's surgery, plus several weeks for recovery. He needed time for healing and to get ready to go back to school. I prepared all my lesson plans for my future substitute since I knew I would be off work for at least three weeks. Fortunately, the timing was in our favor. He had three weeks after surgery for recovery, which lead up to our full week off for Thanksgiving break. I was able to stay home with him for four weeks. Unfortunately this surgery was scheduled for October 31st. Halloween. He loved Halloween.

I grew up going trick-or-treating as a kid, and it was something I looked forward to every year. It was exciting to pick out a new costume. Back in my day, it was usually a cheap plastic mask from K-Mart that smelled funny. In my kindergarten year, I was Lucy from Charlie Brown, so my costume was a mask of her face with the garment made of cheap material of her body to wear over my clothes. The next year, my mom dressed me up like a gypsy. I felt giddy because she let me wear a lot of her costume jewelry. She put me in a black blouse and skirt that belonged to her and was many sizes too big, and safety pinned it to stay on. She also had the black lacy shawl she wrapped around my shoulders, put a bandanna in my hair, and blacked out one of my front teeth. I had no idea what a gypsy was, but I had fun dressing up as one.

I have a few memories of my granddaddy taking my sister and me trick-or-treating in their neighborhood. But there was this particular year I remember vividly. I was in the seventh grade, so my sister was in fifth. My granddaddy told us he was taking us trick-or-treating. I felt so embarrassed because I was too old to be trick-or-treating. He took us down to the local five and dime store to buy a cheap, plastic mask. There were hardly any left, so my sister picked out a black cat, and I got whatever was left...a devil mask...how lovely.

Steve and I carried on the tradition of Halloween fun: choosing a costume, going door to door, learning how to say *"trick or treat!"* and *"thank you"* as soon as the homeowner dropped a piece or two of candy into the pumpkin bucket. It was a bonus when an extra generous homeowner gave handfuls of candy or other cool treats!

This Halloween would be quite different than any other because there would be no trick or treating...so we *thought*.

My friend Heather, who was now a school counselor, approached me with a proposition.

"Would it be okay if we had a trick or treat here at the school for Logan? It would be after school is out, and all the teacher's kids can trick-or-treat with him too. They can go from classroom to classroom, in their costumes."

"Oh my gosh, are you serious?" That would be so special! It took no second thought to accept this proposition. We took the boys to shop for costumes, and Logan chose to be Luke Skywalker from Star Wars, and Landon wanted to be Darth Vader. We bought each of their costumes along with light sabers. It was scheduled...surgery *and* trick-or-treating.

The day before surgery, the kids changed into their costumes right after school to get ready to trick or treat. We played the Star Wars theme song over the PA system. I thought it was rather fitting for a master Jedi. Steve brought our new video camera to film while the kids walked from classroom to classroom and opened their little sacks to receive candy from all the teachers and staff.

It occurred to me how lucky we were to have these wonderful teachers going out of their way to help our little boy feel some joy before another big surgery.

As we were leaving, Heather walked with us out to our car.

"I have something for you," she said. She handed me a basket with snacks, magazines, books, blankets, and cards. As we looked at each other and hugged, I felt my fake *everything's-going-to-be-ok smile sweep across my face*. She started to cry...then I started to cry.

I patted her back and said, "it's going to be okay."

"How is it that *you* are the one consoling *me*?" she asked as we giggled a little. Truthfully, I said it so I could also hear it out loud for myself.

We headed home and began our routine of getting ready for all the pre-op appointments for the next day.

The following morning, we drove to Dallas and went for all of the usual team visits: blood work, media for pictures, anthropology for bone measurements, radiology for MRI and/or CT's, child life services (which we didn't always get) and last but not least, the craniofacial surgeon. All of the appointments went well as expected, and everything was set for surgery the next day.

That evening, I drove to my parents' house to drop off Landon to stay while Logan was in the hospital.

"Landon, you're going to have a sleepover at Maw Maw and Paw Paw's house while Logan has surgery on his head. He's going to be okay, but Mommy and Daddy need to stay with him while he is in the hospital.

"Is it gonna hurt him?" his sweet voice asked.

"No, he will be asleep the whole time, and the doctors will give him medicine so his boo-boo doesn't hurt." I love you, and I will call and talk to you on the phone, okay?"

"Okay, sure," he replied acceptingly.

3 A.M. Sure Comes too Soon

The alarm sounded at 3 a.m., since we had a two hour drive to Dallas. Early surgeries require you to arrive at least two hours prior, kind of like when you're getting ready to go to the airport, except it's not a fun-filled vacation awaiting you, even though you have a few bags packed.

The surgery was scheduled for 7:30 a.m. and we were all ready to go by 4 a.m. We scooped Logan out of bed in his pajamas, loaded up the car, and headed out into the dark morning for the drive to the hospital. We arrived on time, got registered, and checked in, ready to go.

They gave Logan the usual I.V. cocktail of Versed, aka "goofy juice," and let him pick out a movie to watch on a portable DVD player. The routine was usually Steve and me answering the same questions for the surgical nurse and anesthesiologist. Then, the surgeon came to visit Logan and us and asked if he, or we, had any last-minute questions, and explained what to expect. We didn't have anything else to ask...we had been around this block a time or two.

I tried to prepare Logan a little more before this surgery since it was his first one to have, now being a little bit older. This would most likely be the first surgery he would have any memory of, so we wanted to make it as pleasant as possible, however possible that was.

I brought books, old ones and new ones, to read to him while he was recovering. Typically for this surgery, they have to place two dissolvable stitches in each eyelid to sew them shut to protect them. His eyes would often swell up like plums for the first forty-eight hours, which is the peak of swelling.

One of the hardest parts is when your six-year-old child waking up from anesthesia is unable to see anything, even when you explained it prior. It can be quite traumatic.

Logan was always very anxious coming out of anesthesia and would thrash and cry a lot. I can only imagine how scary, overwhelming, and panic-stricken he must feel waking up in pain, uncomfortable, and unable to see.

The week before the surgery, I prepared Logan with some communication phrases. Although he was capable of communicating, he still struggled with expressing his feelings, especially after surgeries. I wanted to give him some tools to minimize his anxiety in the best way possible. This way, his needs were being met without us and the medical staff, having to probe him, or guessing his needs if he was thrashing around and crying.

"Logan, you know when we talked the other day about you having surgery soon?"

He shook his head in agreement.

"Well, you know you will be asleep the whole time and won't feel a thing, right?"

"Yeah."

"Ok...well, when you wake up your eyes will be swollen shut, so you won't be able to see us, but it is normal, and it will only last a few days. So, when you wake up, just remember these things I am telling you, and they're only temporary. Also, I want to teach you some phrases so you can tell us what you need. The nurses and Dad and I can help you better, okay?"

"Okay."

" When you can't see, but you need something or need to tell us something, use these phrases: If you are in pain, say *I'm in pain, or my head hurts*. If you need to use the restroom, just say *I need to potty*. If you're hungry or thirsty, say *I'm hungry or I'm thirsty*. If you need us close, say *I need a hug*. If you want to move around, say *I want a wagon ride*. I know it probably feels weird and scary not being able to see when you wake up, but it's normal for this surgery and won't last forever. Dad and I will remind you too. So I want you to repeat these phrases to me out loud so you can remember them."

While we were in the surgery holding room, I reviewed everything we discussed, asking him which phrase would he use for each need, and he knew them all by heart.

Once again, we hugged and kissed our boy, said our *I love you,* and the gurney rolled away. I thought it would be easier this time, but it wasn't. Every time I watch the gurney roll away, the wound in my heart reopens.

We headed to the waiting room to sit with our parents.

"Do you want anything from the cafeteria? Dad and I are going downstairs to get breakfast," Steve asked.

"No, when y'all get back, your mom and my mom and I will go downstairs to get coffee."

Five hours later the surgeon came out and discussed how the surgery went.

"He did very well, and he has some growth room now. Once the nurses get him set up in the ICU, someone will come get you. They usually called me into the ICU pretty quickly after they had wheeled him in there to help get him settled down and hooked up. He needed to hear my voice so I could explain he was okay and we were all there for him.

The doctor prescribed medication to help keep him calm in the bed and help with anxiety, but he still had some anxiety attacks. I reminded him of our phrases he could use to express his needs.

After everything, we journeyed into the home stretch. Usually, after the forty-eight hours pass, the doctor comes in and removes the stitches from his eyelids. For him to be able to see a little more each day as the swelling goes down was like another race finished.

After the dust settled, he had a few nights of stabilization. The nurses said his blood work looked good, so the doctor signed orders for us to be moved out of PICU. *Regular* rooms were indicative of wagon rides, playroom visits, and sometimes visits from therapy dogs. It was the biggest sense of relief...he was *safe* now. It also meant we were another step closer to going home. When the tiny slit in his eyelid began to barely peek open, his spirit came alive again. The wagon rides around the children's floor were always a hit.

Logan was healing quickly, so it he was once again ready for discharge. Another one down for the record!

Chapter 15
School Daze, More Diagnoses,
and Brotherly Shenanigans

"Everybody is a genius. But if you judge a fish by its ability to climb a tree, it will live its whole life believing that it is stupid."

~ *Albert Einstein*

I knew we had some challenges once Logan finished Kindergarten and was a few months into First Grade. He did fairly well with academics, as far as letters and numbers, etc. However, he struggled with focus and was physically active all the time. I mentioned my concerns at his well-child check-up, but his pediatrician at the time wanted to first rule out any learning disabilities before pursuing any ADD/ADHD diagnoses.

This was a catch twenty-two. On one hand, we have to wait and make sure that Logan doesn't have learning disabilities so that we don't explore medication options prematurely. On the other hand, schools do not typically test for learning disabilities this young, since most kids learn at different paces, and being that young, school administrators are required to do a plethora of intervention and document, which can take up to a year or longer. It felt to me like the old dilemma: *which came first, the chicken or the egg?*

First grade came around, so we decided to see how this school year went. He struggled a lot, mainly with being still so he could focus and he was always fidgeting with something in his hands, whether it was a tiny ball of play dough or an eraser.

One day his first-grade teacher approached me after school. My resource classroom was right down the hallway from Logan's first-grade class.

"Hey Lisa, I need to talk to you about Logan." My stomach flipped. *Oh, man. This doesn't sound good. I am not prepared for this.*

"Ok, sure, what's up?" I asked her pretending to not have a clue what she wanted to talk to me about.

"Um, I had to write a behavior report on Logan today. He and another friend were running around the room chasing each other laughing and spanking each other."

Well...neat. My kid is spanking other children.

"Okay, I will talk to him about keeping his hands to himself. Thank you for letting me know."

With a chuckle she replied, "just to let you know, I think he is a very sweet boy, and I mean that."

"Thank you for saying that. And, thank you for having patience with him while we figure out what is best for him," I sheepishly replied.

It wasn't long after this incident that I brought up the subject again with the pediatrician. She stood by her previous recommendation of testing for a learning disability, but this time gave us a referral to Scottish Rite Hospital where they would do a full evaluation, and it was free of charge.

I took a day off from work and drove him to Scottish Rite Hospital in Dallas. I had been there once before, back when Logan was only about seven or eight months old where we had x-rays done of his hands and feet before releasing his fingers and toes. I sat in a waiting area while the diagnostician took him back for a couple of hours and did several cognitive and academic tests on him. She came out with him and let him pick out a free book that he could take home.

"Mrs. Brown, I can talk to you now about the results. If you and Logan will follow me into my office we can go over everything," she stated.

We followed her like she asked and sat down. Within five minutes she explained that Logan is displaying some attention deficits with inattentiveness.

As I suspected.

"Here is a copy of my report that you can take back to the doctor, your copy, as well as a third copy to share with his school if you choose to do so."

Ok, here we go. Another thing. Just stay positive Lisa, lots of people struggle with this. My mantra now changed to, Lord help him behave in school. He already has attention brought to him because he looks different, but now he acts differently.

Times were hard. Steve had just come back home about six months prior, was adjusting to living back at home, and our house was on the market again.

Steve had a hard time understanding and quite frankly accepting the ADHD diagnosis in the beginning, and he was against medication...at first. He didn't have a lot of knowledge of the condition and believed that our son was just being unruly. In his defense, he's never really been around, nor experienced anyone with ADHD. His graduating class was thirty-two. I also understood the controversy and trepidations on medication.

After some time though, through articles, learning from other parents, and me relentlessly explaining to him that he wasn't purposefully being disobedient, he was simply *wired* differently, he started understanding. The best way I could describe it to him was that it was like other conditions in our body. If you have high blood pressure, you're going to treat it. If you have a heart condition, you're going to treat it. But sadly, when you have a *wiring and processing* condition involving your brain and mental health, it is viewed negatively. Yes, both heart and blood pressure conditions are life threatening and must be treated to sustain a healthy life. But, shouldn't the brain also be treated accordingly, with the same importance to live a functional life? If we have impulse control issues, processing deficits, and/or the inability to focus, then how can we sustain a job? Not everyone with ADHD requires medication, but some do in in order to sustain a functional life.

Management of these conditions is so important whether through cognitive behavioral therapy, medication, or both.

****

Accommodations and Modifications

Beginning in second grade, I tried a lot of different things at home to help him with some of his physical struggles. For example, I bought a special keyboard for the computer that had extra-large keys with black letters. For one, they were easier for him to see the letters with the reversed coloring, and the larger keys were better for his fingers. I took it to school for the teacher to borrow, in which she plugged it into her computer and allowed him to use it for spelling tests.

Written expression became his nemesis, and from second grade on it became more difficult as the demand for written work increased. But, despite his physical mobility and with loads of occupational therapy and hard work, Logan learned how to spell and write.

Although he knew *how* to write, the question was whether he *should.* He would come home with blisters and calluses between his fingers, and sometimes they would bleed. He adaptively held the writing utensil because he was unable to physically bend his fingers, so there was extra pressure between his fingers.

Modifications and accommodations were added to his educational plan, for him to be allowed to use assistive technology for longer written assignments. First, they provided him with an iPad, then he was eventually assigned a laptop to use at all times.

Sometimes our children's baby steps are their marathons.

****

Brotherly Shenanigans

As the years passed and the boys grew, there were never any dull moments with them. They played, argued, and fought together with the best of them. *Normal* brother behavior. They loved swimming, riding their bikes, jumping on the trampoline, playing video games, and watching movies – the things we called staple entertainment because they were guaranteed to have fun.

I was out shopping with my mom, now seven-year-old Logan, and four-year-old Landon. We went to the store to shop for some new clothes for me. I had changed teaching positions and was about to begin a seven-year journey at a new campus, the same one where my children would go for elementary school through the sixth grade.

I knew they sold some ladies' casual clothing, and that was exactly what I was looking for. Landon had been riding in the shopping buggy and Logan was walking, but they wanted to switch. So, as Mommies do, they do whatever they need to in order to get their shopping or tasks done. My mom was pushing the buggy while I was looking at some casual skirts that they had on sale and I was showing my mom when all of a sudden we heard Logan burst out into a peal of very loud laughter. It was the kind of laughter that is almost forced, where everyone looks at you to control your kid because they are being too loud or rambunctious in the store.

Low and behold, there was Logan in the basket staring at his four-year-old brother, who had taken it upon himself to stand behind a nude mannequin with his arms around her from behind, dancing a jig, with his little hands placed perfectly on her plastic bosom.

I sucked in a whiff of air, placed my hand on my forehead and closed my eyes. "Oh my gosh."

My mom looked over and saw what was happening and couldn't stifle her laughter. Initially, I was embarrassed. My four-year-old boy was entertaining his brother by groping a nude mannequin in the middle of a department store, right on the aisle where people were walking by.

Neat. I bet this looks like a real treat to all these other customers walking by. To all you customers witnessing this: I promise Steve and I don't act like this at home...well, at least not me, anyway.

It totally caught me off guard. Then after I ushered him back over to our buggy, we shuffled off to the register where I was ready to pay for my items.

My mom and I loaded the boys into the car along with our packages, and then looked at each other and could no longer hold in our laughter. I asked a rhetorical question, "Did my kid really just feel up that mannequin?" My mom's only reply through her laughter and tears was, "Yes I believe he did."

****

Landon seemed to take on the *big brother* role, helping and encouraging Logan along the way. He was quite precocious and innately had a servant's heart. They argued one moment, and were pals the next. But Logan didn't mind asking him for help, and he was glued to Landon's hip, especially when we went places. I think he knew that Landon was always his guardian and would protect him if anyone made any snarky remarks in public. Likewise, Landon filled the role. I could tell there were times when he didn't want to, but he did anyway. When you're the big brother or sister, you don't want them always tagging along.

****

Setbacks and successes were equivocal in our days. Surgeries inevitably set back Logan's learning since it took at least eight weeks for a full recovery, counting the decrease in swelling of his head. Nonetheless, he seemed to catch up rather quickly.

His personality began to change somewhat between third and fourth grade. This was the age where he truly noticed differences between him and other students' appearances. He had one friend in school that was always there for him, so Logan clung to him like a dryer sheet.

With Landon, he was a social butterfly. He made friends easily and loved helping people. I knew the day would come when Landon might excel past Logan, but wasn't sure how it would play out. At first, Landon became frustrated and irritated with Logan's maturity level not being the same as his. So, again, this was another *big (little) brother* role he took on. But, over time, as they both matured, Landon understood where Logan was coming from.

Landon taught me how to laugh again. I read an article about siblings of a child with special needs. It pointed out how they were way beyond their years in maturity, especially ones with medical complexities. They are intuitive, sensitive, and put others before themselves. They like to make their parents smile or laugh because they've seen the heartache.

This made perfect sense. Landon knew more medical terms than most adults. Even though he might have lacked some attention at times during our hospital stays with Logan, he was and is never on my back burner.

****

I approached Steve one evening after dinner with a discussion of church.

"I think it's a good time now to try and find a church for us to attend. Logan is a little older and his ADHD medication is helping, so hopefully he would be okay in kid's church. There's a church I attended a few times with a friend when I was young, we could try that one first, since it's close. What do you think?"

"Yeah, we really need to. Maybe Logan could make friends too."

We tried the mentioned church. Steve came a few times, but often was working twelve-hour shifts. Logan had immense anxiety when going to new places, at least without being by my side. I took the boys to the children's center for kid's church so I could sit during the adult sermon.

"Can I stay with Landon?" Logan asked me, glued to my side.

"Let me ask."

We walked into the classroom for Kindergarteners, and Landon walked right in with no trepidations to look around. "This is Logan, Landon's brother. Would it be okay if he stayed with his brother since this is his first time?"

"No I'm sorry, we don't combine grade or age levels. He needs to go with the other third graders."

Wow. Seriously? Come on, lady. This is church. You have no idea how hard it was just to GET him here. Make him your helper or something.

My face flushed with disappointment.

Landon stayed in the classroom, and Logan went with me to the sermon.

We went into the sanctuary and sat in one of the back pews.

He squirmed and fidgeted the entire time. I really wished he would go to the kid's church.

We tried again the next Sunday, and Logan would not budge to go into the kid's church classroom. So, Landon stayed in his classroom, and Logan and I went to sermon.

About halfway through, Logan leaned over and whispered, "I feel like I'm going to throw up."

Oh my. I don't want him to throw up everywhere here in the chapel.

I took him by the hand and we stood up quietly to walk to the back door. We made it outside and sat on the steps for a minute.

"Does your tummy still hurt? I asked

"A little," he replied.

I could tell that this wasn't a tummy bug.

Sigh. I think this is more anxiety than anything else. I looked at the time on my phone, and church was about to be dismissed.

"Well, let's go get Landon and go home."

If this is how it's going to be, then I don't even want to go either. I just don't need any more emotional roller coasters. All I want is for my children to have a normal life. I want to go places without people staring at him, without anxiety...for all of us.

I told Steve about the situation. He responded the same way I had felt.

"Why didn't they just let him go with him the first time?" he asked annoyed.

"I don't know. It's not like Logan was a teenager going into a Kindergarten classroom. They are only three years apart. Regardless, I didn't really get a warm and fuzzy feeling. This just wasn't the church for us.

****

We waited approximately six months before we tried another church. One day Logan had a flyer in his backpack from school that

173

announced a youth basketball program called Upward. I had heard so many positive things about this program, one being it was Christian-based and they gleaned some lessons and verses from the Bible.

One evening, I drove the boys to sign-ups. When we arrived, Logan looked around, and with conviction in his voice said, "I don't want to do this. I changed my mind."

"Are you sure? It will be fun! They will teach you how to play." I pleaded.

"No, I don't want to."

Landon spoke up, "Mommy, can I play?"

"Sure! Let's go see if they have a group for your age." I replied, hoping maybe if Logan saw his brother sign up, he might decide to give it a try.

"Landon, they have signups for your age!"

"Okay, Mommy, I want to play," he said in his sweet five-year-old voice.

"Alright, let's get you signed up!"

That was our first wink from God. We met the coach at the first practice, and it turned out that he was the pastor of the church. He also had a son that was in Landon's class at school. His wife was so kind as well, and walked over to introduce herself to me. I felt her warm kindness immediately. This led us to visiting the church. As it turned out, I saw several people I had graduated high school with.

Months later, we followed this pastor when he began his own church, The Journey Church. We were meeting in an elementary school cafeteria then moved into a church building that became available. What I loved the most is that from the moment we attended, we were treated with open arms and loved like family. We never felt judged, gawked at, and a bonus was that kid's church was a classroom for fourth grade and under! Logan and Landon got to be together. The boys jumped up with excitement when the announcement came, "Kids fourth grade and under, go ahead and make your way to the classroom." They made a beeline for the class.

I'm not gonna lie, I was excited too. This meant I could have some peaceful time, learning from God's word, with no distractions. It was a clear answer. This was going to be our church home.

Finding a church home helped us get back to our beliefs. Beautiful messages reminded us that we didn't have to figure everything out ourselves and solve our own problems. Hearing about God's love and devotion chiseled away the burdens, one chunk at a time. Yes, it was our responsibility to step up to this *test* we had been given. What we lost sight of was the understanding we didn't have to do it alone. One day in church, I couldn't stop the tears from flowing. I made the decision that I was ready to be baptized.

I was forty-one years old when I was baptized. I realized you can never be too old to get baptized, and I hoped that my example would leave a memory for my children seeing their mom make the commitment. The congregation loved me, supported me and cheered me on.

Finally, understanding that God loved me with all my faults, was a game changer for me.

Chapter 16
The Doozy

"Rejoice in hope, be patient in tribulation, be constant in prayer."
~ Romans 12:12 (ESV)

2011

I wanted to dig my heels in the sand. Immaturity jolted through me like a proverbial three year old who had misbehaved and refused to walk to time-out. I felt I might need an escort to the corner, provoking them to drag me by my arms, all the while digging my heels into the floor, then kicking and screaming: "No, I don't want to go!" My "what if's" overflowed like a broken dam.

The surgery I dreaded since this sweet boy was born was now on the horizon. If there was anything positive about this situation, it was the timing of this surgery. It was set for May 5th, and I was so thankful he would be off from school for the month of May then have the summer to heal.

Although the surgeon had prepared us in the beginning for this future surgery, no words or advice could have prepared us for what lurked ahead. It predicted change to his appearance but was warranted for a few reasons.

First of all, his airway was compromised. He was a complete mouth breather because his midfacial bones were compressing his nasal airway, in addition to having partially closed nasal passages. After several of his sleep studies, it was determined he had mild to moderate sleep apnea.

Secondly, his eyes bulged, which put him at high risk for injury to the eye. Typically, kids with Apert Syndrome are born with very shallow orbits (the hollowed-out area of the skull where the eyeballs

"

rest). Because of this, he needed special bowed lenses in his glasses. It was hard to find sunglasses that fit properly and wouldn't touch his eyeballs, or at minimum smash his eyelashes. He was extremely sensitive to light, so we chose transition lenses for his vision glasses.

Lastly, it would give him a more typical appearance, helping him in school and life. I honestly didn't want him to change in appearance. I loved him for the way he looked. But as described to us, I knew this surgery was a necessity. My main concern was helping his airway and protecting his eyes and brain.

My feelings of ambiguity confused me. Undoubtedly, fear swallowed me up like Jonah and the whale, throwing anxiety into high gear. I began doubting myself as a mother when questions poked at me, like: *"is it okay for me to feel sad? I love his face just the way it is and I really don't want it to change."* Or, *"is it okay for me to feel happy and hopeful that he is getting a new face? Perhaps this would help in his years to come since social acceptance relies so much on appearance these days."*

How am I supposed to feel? How was he going to feel? Will this scare him? Will he like the new look he will have?

These questions haunted me.

****

The name of this necessary surgery was a *midface advancement.* I didn't want to fathom what this entailed. The protocol for this grave surgery was attaching a "halo" device into the sides of his skull with titanium screws, and attaching a dental splint to the pallet of his mouth right behind his front teeth. This came with tools for *us* to turn twice a day for four weeks, which allowed the bones to be pulled forward in millimeters each day.

In the months leading up to the surgery, we were educated on what the device looked like, how long he would wear it, and where it would be attached.

We began talking to him about this surgery a few weeks before the actual date, but we really weren't sure what to say. How do you explain to your son that he has to have another surgery on his head, but this time he will come out looking significantly different?

Our sweet son was only nine years old, so we felt telling him too early before the procedure would not be in his best interest. Secondly, we decided that waiting until the time was closer would be best for him because we didn't want to scare him and add any "additional" anxiety.

Preparations were as usual, with the exceptions of a few things. I bought Logan some short sleeved button up shirts since he wouldn't be able to pull a shirt over his head. I also bought him a pillow filled with microbeads. I presumed it would have a little more *give* than his regular pillow. We did anything we could think of to make him as comfortable as possible.

On the day before surgery, I drove Logan to Dallas for his pre-op appointments with the craniofacial team. We arrived in Dallas with a couple of hours to spare before our first appointment, so I stopped at Barnes & Noble so Logan could pick out some books he wanted us to read to him.

He picked out two books: *The One and Only Ivan, by Katherine Applegate, and Guinea Dog, by Patrick Jennings,* our go-to choice for story time.

****

When we arrived at the hospital, our first stop was to see the media department, which seemed so much more relevant this time.

"Ok, let's take these photos. Logan, go ahead," Max, the media photographer stopped mid-sentence.

Logan had already sat down in the chair and pulled his shoes off. That's usually what they had him do because they take photos of his hands and feet as well.

"Haha, I guess you already know the routine, huh?" he said.

I stood over to the side and held his glasses while they took pictures. His assistant rotated him on the swiveling chair, from left to right, getting different angles. Then she had him lean back to get an upward profile view.

Poof! Then flash. "Okay now turn and look at the Elmo sticker on the wall." Another, *poof*, then, *flash*. "Great job, Logan, you are doing so well!"

We walked into the office for the last appointment of the day, which was usually with the surgeon.

"Hi. Please go ahead and complete this paperwork, and the doctor will be with you shortly," the receptionist advised.

Fifteen minutes later, Dr. Fearon opened the door.

"Hi, Logan! Come on back," he greeted.

We followed him back to his office, where he asked Logan to sit in a chair by his desk. I sat down in a chair across from the doctor's desk. He took some measurements of his skull.

The doctor pulled out a metal device with purple on the sides and began explaining what it was to Logan.

"Logan. See this device? We call it a halo, and it's what I'm going to attach to your head so we can move the bones in your face to help you breathe better and protect your eyes. These screws on each side will go in your skull on the sides of your head. This other bar you see in the front will be inserted under your top teeth in the gums. But, the good news is that you will be asleep the whole time, so you won't feel a thing. Would you like to hold it?" he asked.

Logan nodded yes and took the halo from the doctor and inspected it.

He handed it back to the doctor and allowed me to have a turn.

"Mom, do you have any questions?" the doctor asked.

"Yes, actually. I made a list so I wouldn't forget," I replied, pulling out the yellow legal pad displaying my long list of the following questions:

1. *Is this surgery called the Le Fort III, or R.E.D, I've heard it called both (rigid external device)?*
2. *Will they be mailing the pre-op and surgery itinerary?*
3. *Will he be placed on a ventilator? I'm really scared about this.*
4. *Will he be able to chew at all?*
5. *Will the neurosurgeon be involved at all with this surgery?*
6. *Can I be there right when he wakes up? He has severe anxiety, perhaps I can help talk him through it so that the nurses can get him hooked up and settled easier.*
7. *How will he be able to sleep? Can he sleep on his sides? I worry about the screws that will be in his skull.*
8. *What about teeth brushing?*
9. *Will this affect his speech?*
10. *Do we need to buy anything special for this?*

He answered one question at a time.

"These are some great questions. I will be using the Le Fort III, which will gradually advance the bones in his mid-face. You will use this tool to make turns once a day for four weeks, then the device remains attached another four weeks to allow the bone to fill in and set.

You will get all the pre-op information a week prior. As far as the ventilator, my plan is to not put him on one, unless his airway is compromised. In this case, I will perform a tracheostomy to aid his breathing. The neurosurgeon will not be in this surgery because we are not removing any bone. He will not be able to chew in the beginning, so he should only have liquids for the first few weeks. I've heard from some of my patients that after about three weeks they are able to chew soft foods, but for others they remain on liquids. His speech may be affected due to the stent placed inside his gums under his front teeth, but he will still be able to talk. You can still brush his teeth, but a water flosser might help as well.

He can sleep like he normally sleeps, so if he is a side sleeper, then he can sleep on his side. He will adapt and sleep however is comfortable for him and he won't be in any pain. As we wake him from the surgery, I will start him on a medication that will keep him in sort of a "twilight" state, but not so heavy it keeps him knocked out. This will help ease any anxiety."

On the way home, we had asked Logan if he had any questions about it, and his main one was "is it gonna hurt?" So we reiterated what the doctor had told him, because frankly, we still wondered the same thing. The doctor explained to him that it would not hurt, he might be a little sore and tender around the skin areas where the screws went into his skull, but he would be asleep and wouldn't feel anything. He would wake up and have his super hero halo on.

I worried. I worried a lot actually, especially since Logan has never been precise at expressing his feelings verbally. Words became lost in translation.

There was a time when the teacher's aide in his Kindergarten class giggled as she told me he would walk up to her and hand her his glasses without a word. He did the same thing at home. I knew he wanted his lenses on his glasses cleaned, and ironically I think he expected others to know it too without having to tell you. I constantly asked him to "use your words" and after multiple tries of having him use his words, he would tell me 'clean 'em.'" When the teacher's aide told me this, I got tickled. I know she probably thought I did everything for him without making him talk, but it truly wasn't the case. This was his epic strong willed personality shining through. She and I giggled though, because she told me one day he walked up to her and handed his glasses, and she stood there. I think she told him, *hi* or something, or *I don't know what that means.*

Often when he had surgeries he would often thrash about in his bed in the ICU coming out of the anesthesia while they were trying to get him all hooked up to monitors, adjust his catheter, take his temperature, move his pillows, check his IV, take blood, etc. He struggled with communicating to us what his actual needs were. I knew he was uncomfortable and most likely in pain, not to mention the frustration of not being able to see because his eyes had two stitches in each eyelid to keep them shut. The surgeon sutured his eyelids, not only to protect the eyes during surgery, but it was explained that swelling can be so severe where there have been cases of children's eyelids sliding back behind the eyeball which is very dangerous.

I sat down with him and reminded him that after his surgery, his eyes would be swollen shut for a few days.

"They will give you medicine if you are in pain, but let's review those phrases you can say to me, Dad, or the nurses and doctors when you are uncomfortable or need something, okay?"

"Okay."

We reviewed the urgent phrases like: *I'm hurting; I'm thirsty or hungry; I need to use the restroom; I need a hug.*

We came up with additional phrases for his needs for when we were released from the ICU to a regular room: *I want a wagon ride; read me a story; I want to go to the playroom; I want to watch a movie.*

After the other surgeries, I chomped at the bit, waiting to be notified when it was finished, yet had butterflies in my stomach because I knew how much stress lay ahead. The usual routine was: after the surgery they would inform us of how it went and details of any "extra" things that had to be fixed or repaired, then they would tell us to head upstairs to the third floor to the next waiting room, which was the waiting area for the ICU. Once I got there, I knew I could talk to him and he would hear my voice, and I would do my best to calm him down. Once everything calmed down, family could take turns coming in to give him love and say hi to him. After that, I was on my mommy radar for 24 hours at a time.

This time felt different. It wasn't a *one and done* kind of deal. We were dealing with encumbered attachments, tools, feeding tube, and diet changes. This unfamiliar territory was unnerving, and frankly seems barbaric. This one's a doozy.

****

A week prior to the surgery, I was in a meeting with both my principal and assistant principal. I changed teaching positions to be the campus' Intervention Specialist, helping teachers with struggling students. I also worked with small groups of students identified with Dyslexia and/or learning disabilities. Every week we held meetings consisting of the administrators, counselors, classroom teachers, and myself. The purpose of the meetings was to discuss each student's progression or regression and devise a plan.

This particular week marked one week prior to surgery. My anxiety was at peak, and felt my chest tighten as the time grew nearer.

I'm very fortunate for the fact that I was friends with my administrators, and worked with amazing teachers at my campus. It was the very reason why I wanted my children to go to school with me. I knew all the teachers.

While we were sitting in my office, these ladies took one look at my face and asked with grave concern how I was handling everything.

Upon explaining this surgery, my lip quivered, and my voice broke. I was trying to speak, but couldn't through my sobbing. A teacher walked in for the first meeting, and my principal turned to her and said, "This meeting has been canceled. We will get with you later."

I continued sharing the details, while trying to catch my breath. They cried with me and reassured me, "Lisa, if you need anything, please let us know. Don't worry about work, just take care of your family and yourself. We will be praying for Logan and for your family."

I realized how lucky I was from the comfort of their words, to know my administrators were understanding of my situation, and most importantly would pray for us. As a distraught mother, I longed for it. I sought their encouragement and comfort because I had no idea what would happen. Not everyone has an employer who empathizes and understands when you need to take off so much time. Although it didn't remove the stress waiting ahead, it comforted me to work around such loving people.

I knew it was time to tell my coworkers about my situation. A handful already knew, but they didn't know the extent of it, so I informed them the best way I could...I wrote a letter.

****

LETTER TO MY COWORKERS

Dear FAA, (Fine Arts Academy)

I wanted to share some personal information with you regarding an upcoming event in May. For those of you who don't know what Logan's syndrome is, it is called Apert syndrome, which requires numerous surgeries throughout his life until he becomes an adult. (His skull and facial bones do not grow with the rest of him, thus causing no room for brain growth and possible airway blockage). Logan is scheduled to have another surgery on May 6th for a midface advancement. This is much different than the one he had in 2008 and there is so much involved in this process, but in a nutshell, they are going to surgically implant a rigid external device called a LeFort III underneath his facial bones from the top of his brow down to his upper jaw. The bones will be cut and attached to this device, and we will have to turn this device with a special tool every day to gradually move his facial bones out. The turning will be done for four weeks, then he will wear the device for another four weeks for the bone matter to set. I know this sounds very graphic, but that is exactly what it is.

This is a surgery that we've known he would need since he was born, and dreaded more than any other, but the doctors say that the time has come. The reasons for this surgery are first and foremost: to help improve his breathing, help protect his eyes, and improve his speech as he will have a more typical structure of alignment, and also improve his appearance. I am being very direct in this letter, but have been on an emotional roller coaster with everything that is involved with this surgery. Logan does NOT know about his upcoming surgery yet, as we have chosen not to tell him until the time is right. I do not mind if you discuss this among your teammates, but I do ask that you please, please make sure that there are NO children around and also that you please NOT share this with your own children as well, at least until after the surgery date.

Normally I am VERY open and honest with any questions. However, it is very hard for me to discuss details about the surgery right now as the date is getting closer and closer.

I have spoken with Mrs. Stark, and she will address this with the third grade students while Logan is out for surgery and recovery. His appearance will change, but we do not know how much.

There is a website called "CaringBridge" for families and patients, where we will be setting up a webpage for Logan, so that we can communicate with family and friends during the day, and post updates, comments, etc. This will be available for you to visit if you wish, and when we get this set up, I will give you the log in directions where you can check for updates on the surgery, recovery, and/or post comments yourself.

I will be out of the office beginning May 4th, and will not return until May 30th for the last week of school. My mom will be coming over to stay with him allowing me to finish out the school year to help financially. Logan will not be returning until the beginning of next school year.

Steve and I are firm believers in God and prayer, and know that He will be with us during these trying times. Nonetheless, they will be very difficult. Any prayers will be welcomed and appreciated ☺

> *Sincerely,*
> *Lisa Brown*

****

The next letter I wrote was to all of third grade. I sat there at the computer, staring at the screen. I envisioned all their little faces, as they would be told these details. How do I tell these kids about this? I don't want to be too graphic because they are still so young, and I don't want to scare them. On the other hand, I have to prepare them for seeing a different kid next year in fourth grade and they will naturally have questions. The only way I know how to accomplish this is to simply speak from my heart. Lord, please give me the right words...

****

LETTER TO THIRD GRADE

Dear Third Grade,

Most of you know who Logan Brown is in Mrs. Brannon's class and he is so lucky to have many of you as his dear friends! I want to share some information with you about why he will be absent for the rest of the school year.

You are all third graders, (almost fourth graders!) and probably already know that "we are all made different..." and some of us are made a little more differently than others. Logan might look a little different than most of you, but he still has a smart brain, a loving heart, and feelings just like you and I. Logan's doctors say that he needs to have surgery now, on the bones in his face to help protect his beautiful eyes, and to help him breathe better.

As his Mom, I wanted to share all of this with you so that you can understand what is going on. I also want you to know that he is very strong and brave, and that he is going to be okay. He will be home to recover and regain his strength because he can't wait to be a big fourth grader!! When fourth grade begins next year, Logan will come back to school like all of you, and may look different than he does now, but he will still be the same brave, loving, caring, Lego-playing boy that we all know. We should all love each other for who we are, and that being unique means that there's no one else like you. WE ARE ALL UNIQUE!!

So in honor of Logan Brown, I am giving you a wristband that says, "Beyond the face is a heart." This means that even though our faces may look different, we still have a heart that has feelings, and loves, and wants to be loved just like you! ☺

Thank you for being kind to him, taking up for him, and just being someone he can call a friend.

Love,

Mrs. Brown (Logan's Mommy :)

Chapter 17
Face to Face

*"Who sees the human face correctly: the photographer,
the mirror, or the painter?"*

~ Pablo Picasso

May 6, 2011

I cried in anticipation of this day for four months. Steve was a workhorse, so he deflected all his worries of this upcoming surgery into his job. Now, it has arrived. Today, they will transform my son's face into a completely different one.

We got ready to leave our house around 4:30 a.m. I made prior arrangements for Landon to stay the night with my parents and then ride with friends to school the next morning.

All of our bags were packed, and we didn't forget Logan's special pillow and his trusty plush puppy, *Rescue.*

Steve was in the living room putting on his shoes when I sat down beside him and could barely utter, "Will you please say a prayer?"

I slipped my hand into his hand, bowed our heads, and shed tears as he prayed. We loaded our stuff in the truck with Logan in tow, still in his pajamas, camouflage robe and slippers. We were Dallas bound in the dark morning hours.

****

We arrived at the hospital and registered at the front desk. They directed us to the second floor, what is now called the *beehive* since the last time we were here. They had remodeled the area that used to be the emergency room, but we didn't know it would be this beautiful new children's wing.

We walked up the stairs to the beehive overlooking registration and the atrium entrance. They sent us to a holding room, which was much more kid-friendly than they used to be. The nurse came in and gave him a hospital gown printed with whales. I helped him change and into the covers of the hospital bed.

When she returned, she brought Logan a freshly warmed blanket. She also had two other blankets, homemade from soft fleece material from the Project Linus foundation. One had spiders and the other had turtles.

"Logan, you get to pick your very own blanket to keep (adding to the collection he has going). Which one would you like?" she asked.

"Spiders," he replied.

"Okay, spiders it is." She laid the blanket over him, and then gave him a portable DVD player to hold and watch movies while waiting to be taken back.

Things had dramatically changed in the hospital since we started this journey, but for the better. The private room assigned us to accommodate most of the family provided a calm and peaceful atmosphere.

The nurse came into the room with another nurse, the *one* who was there to wheel us away, down to the surgery holding room…*the* room with all the beds, hospital curtains, monitors, and cold air.

We played our usual song and dance of hugs and "see you in a little while," after they gave him his usual cocktail of "goofy juice," but as I watched the gurney roll away for the umpteenth time, my grieving process started all over again.

I fell madly in love with this baby boy the first time I was able to hold him. I loved him no matter what, nor what rare condition he had. He was the cutest baby I had ever seen. As he grew to become this nine-year-old, strong-willed boy, I loved the way he was. I couldn't fathom him any other way. Yet now, I *had* to. Emotional ambiguity tapped on each of my shoulders.

I wrapped my arms around Steve, sobbed into his shirt, and prayed some more. I prayed for myself. I had no idea how I was going to mentally and emotionally handle this. I prayed especially for Steve. He internalized everything...*would this break him? Will this break us?* It was hard to process watching your child wheeled back to the operating room, time after time.

Can we handle the emotional stress...again? I wish I had someone to talk to who has been through what we've been through. Someone who knows what this hospital life is like with our own children...someone whose child goes from face to face after this doozy of a surgery.

****

We both walked out of the holding area to head to the waiting room where the rest of our family was along with my friend. The nurse told us to go have breakfast since this was a long surgery, but I couldn't stomach food at this point. I did want some strong coffee though. Coffee is my comfort. It's warm, helps my brain function, and gives me some sort of psychological assurance that everything will be okay.

Steve and the other men left to go eat breakfast in the cafeteria, while the women stayed and drank coffee.

We all sat around in the waiting room, visiting and observing other families in and out. Six hours later, the surgical nurse called us in the waiting room to let us know the surgery was over and all went well. She instructed us to make our way to the third floor of the PICU waiting room, where the doctors would come speak with us.

We made it upstairs, and within twenty minutes, Dr. Fearon walked into the waiting room. The butterflies in my stomach aroused.

"He did great, everything went well. They're getting him comfortable now, so you'll be able to see him in a bit. I have him on a medication keeping him calm, the *twilight* medicine that we discussed. This one allows him to be alert and awake, but not so heavily sedated."

My shoulders lowered. I was so worried about his anxiety, thrashing, and the possibilities of him tugging at the device not remembering or knowing what it is.

I wrapped my arms around Dr. Fearon, even though I knew he wasn't a big "huggy" person, but a lot of doctors aren't. They keep their professionalism intact, and I respect that. But, I couldn't hold back my appreciation, and for me, it's through affection.

"I'll take it," he said and hugged me back.

Steve shook his hand and gave him a quick man-hug as well.

"I'll be by to check on him tomorrow morning," Dr. Fearon said, then walked away in his blue scrubs toward the elevator.

I grabbed Steve before we turned to our family and friends, hugged him, and cried. But, this time, each tear was a representation of something different: relief the surgery went well; relief he will be calm when we walk in; fear of my reaction when I will not recognize my son; the grief of his changed appearance; joy that perhaps he won't get as many stares now with his new face. Yet, there really wasn't time to deal with or process any of these emotions.

As parents, we do a quick change like Clark Kent as he runs into the phone booth as a regular guy, with fears and emotions, yet coming out seconds later as Superman. Except our cool capes to show we would try to save the day were invisible. We become good actresses and actors, in the sense that our feelings are masked by great and brave performances. But, the only way we obtained our *invisible* superhero capes was when God gently laid them across our shoulders and said, "I've got this. I've got you. You will always have me by your side, and I'm sorry you're hurting." So, we put on our stage faces, took a deep breath, and faced the music. *Okay. Now we're ready. It's showtime.*

We released our embrace and walked over to where our family was sitting and shared the news with them. About ten minutes later, one of the ICU nurses came out to get Steve and me. We followed her through the automatic ICU doors and down the hall to his room. The next few moments, which were probably only a few seconds, ran in slow motion for me. I took a deep breath, exhaled, and walked in to see Logan in his hospital bed tilted in a partial upright sitting position, with the halo (R.E.D. – Rigid External Distractor) attached...calm as a cucumber. *Big exhale. Smile. Don't cry. He looks fantastic. He looks so...different. He's not thrashing and crying out in pain! Elation and inundation took hold of my brain. Which one do I allow myself to feel? For right now, it was neither. It's time to be Mommy and nurture this boy to the end of the earth.*

"Hey, buddy! Mommy and Daddy are right here," I said in an excited, but half-whisper, and picked up his hand and stroked it while I held it. "Dr. Fearon said everything went really well, and now you get to rest. Do you need anything right now?"

"Puppy," he replied.

I grabbed Rescue the puppy and placed it under his hands. "He's right here."

I kissed his forehead.

Steve spoke up. "Hey bud, you did great." He patted his leg. "Everyone is wanting to say hi and see you, so I am going to take turns with them since there can only be two people in here at once."

One by one, each grandparent, aunt, uncle, and friend came in to give him encouragement, well wishes, hugs, and kisses. Then one by one, they all departed the hospital to make their way home. This was the hard part for me. Everyone leaves, the dust settles, and the silence allows the reverberation to roar in my head. Clearly, I didn't want everyone staying up at the hospital all night long, but there's comfort in knowing they're out in the waiting room for you when it's your turn to take a walk, get coffee, or sit still for a minute.

After everyone left, and Logan was good and stable, I was ready for something real to eat. By this time of the evening, all of the hospital cafeterias and restaurants were closed, so I asked Steve to run down the street to get us something from the sandwich shop.

After Steve left, Logan was sleeping off and on. The cadence of the machines put me in a trance as I sat by his bedside and stared out at the dark sky. It was so strange to me, seeing the business on the streets outside from the third floor of this pediatric intensive care unit, knowing the whole world was still conducting business as usual. For me, hospital stays felt like time stood still.

I began a silent conversation with God, mostly filled with thanksgiving. Here I am sitting in this hospital, once again witnessing my son enduring another *hard thing,* yet I was grateful. He was doing okay, he was going to *be* okay, and *we* were going to be okay. *We have a long road ahead of us.* As grim and frightful the situation was, a small wave of peace swept across my soul. I felt the prayers. We were so blessed to have amazing doctors to help us in this situation. Only fifty plus years ago, this innovation and medical advancement didn't exist yet, and some lives were lost. Now, here we are. Logan was going to be able to breathe, smell, chew and eat with ease because God created these doctors who are doing what they were born to do: help these children by giving them the most advanced medical treatment necessary to live a full functioning and best quality of life. God is awesome.

****

We weren't allowed to have food in the ICU, so when Steve came back to the room with my food, we tag teamed. Instead of sitting out in the small ICU waiting area, I wanted to go downstairs to the first floor of the children's hospital entrance. It was so beautiful and peaceful there.

I sat down on the long s-shaped couch and stared at the digital aquarium playing on the mounted TV while I ate my sandwich. When I finished, I called my sister so we could finally talk.

I updated her on how Logan was doing, even though my Mom had kept her informed during the day. We chatted for a bit, and it felt good, and *normal*, to hear her voice. Once we hung up, I lay back on the couch. *I just need a few more minutes to breathe.*

I stared up at the three-story ceiling. In the center was a large skylight in the shape of an octagon. Surrounding the window were large butterflies of different colors hanging down from the ceiling, all at different lengths. Standing to the side of the automatic glass entrance doors was a three-story tree with a hollowed-out section to walk through. Neon lights illuminated around the edges of the second floor, changing colors. There was an area with a large caterpillar for kids to climb on and another exit entering into a small outdoor enclosed atrium with foliage and benches. This whole new wing which used to be the hospital's emergency room transformed into a serene and fun children's unit. Quite an improvement since we first started coming here.

I stood up from my meditative state, threw away my trash, and headed back up to the ICU. They allowed us both to stay in his room on the conditions that one of us stays awake, while the other sleeps on the chair. Steve said he would take the first night since he was used to staying awake and working nights. We turned the TV on, volume down, and I laid down to try to sleep for a bit. Logan called for me about every hour, needing something, but mainly begging for a wagon ride already. Unfortunately, we had to break the bad news that wagon rides wouldn't be coming until we moved to a regular room.

****

After three days in the ICU and a couple of days in a regular room, it was time to be discharged from the hospital.

The nurse came in with cans of nutritional supplement, a stethoscope, and extra-large plastic syringes. She taught us how to use the stethoscope to listen in his tummy for air when we pushed on the small syringe.

"When you hear a slight *pft* sound, you know it's still in his stomach and you can now attach the extra-large syringe and fill with the supplement to feed him.

I was apprehensive. *What if I accidentally feed him and the tube has moved up toward his lungs? I can't hear the "pft" sometimes.*

Nevertheless, we learned how to do tube feedings. Baths were a nightmare, as he hated water going over his head as it was, but now more than ever because his head was so sensitive with this barbaric device on. We had to keep it clean though so he wouldn't get an infection at the wound sites.

To help him feel like he was making progress, I had a calendar where we would mark off each day of getting closer to the coveted achievement: removal!

****

We spent most of the time indoors that summer. It was one of the hottest summers we had had in a long time. We almost hit the record from 1980 which racked forty-two days of triple digits, but 2011 took second place with forty days. When we did go outside, the boys played in the sprinkler, ate popsicles, and ice cream.

Over eight weeks of wearing this halo, (the first four weeks of using the tool to make the turns) he endured an unknown complication, requiring another hospital stay.

I'd like to say everything went according to plan, but in the final week of turns, a curveball sped right at us.

The Bloody Scare

In the last week of May, my mom came over to stay with Logan so I could go back and finish out the school year. As a teacher, there are hundreds of things required to "check out" for the summer, plus I needed to finish the week to save on being docked pay. Logan was stable and doing well, so we were comfortable with Mom staying with him during the week.

I was in my bathroom getting ready around 6:30 a.m. I thought I heard Logan's voice. At the time, the house we lived in had split bedrooms with tile throughout the house, so I could hear everything.

"Mommy! Mommy!"

I dropped the can of hairspray and ran out of my bathroom, then made my way to the hallway. Barefoot, I began my short sprint over the tile, until I reached the long trail of blood I had to straddle as I hopped in shock, slowing my steps. I made it to the bathroom where the lights were on and he was standing over the sink. *Oh, sweet Lord.* Blood. Everywhere, there was blood.

"Logan, baby, what happened?" I asked as I tried assessing the situation as best I could, kneeling down to his level.

"I don't know. I woke up and felt all wet by my face," he muttered with his *halo speech.*

"STEVE!" I yelled. "STEVE!"

I got a wet wash rag and began wiping his face, to see if I could tell which area it was coming from.

"Sweetie, did you fall? Here, sit down for a minute. I began wiping the blood from his face, trying to figure out if it was coming from his nose or his mouth.

"No, I just woke up and felt wet, and came in here and turned the lights on and saw blood."

Steve's footsteps patted down the hall, until I heard, "what the heck? What is going on?"

"I don't know. He said he woke up and noticed his face felt all wet. I came in here to this. He must have gotten up, turned on all the lights, and noticed he was bleeding. That's when he yelled for me. I can't tell if it's coming from his mouth or nose."

Logan was alert and lucid, so I handed Steve the washcloth.

"Help him, I'm going to call Dr. Fearon."

I walked to the kitchen and out on the back patio so I could make the call. We didn't get a good cell signal since we lived in the country. I dialed his office and pushed the number to have him paged. It connected me to his answering service, so I explained the situation. The operator took all my information and informed me he would have the doctor paged and call me back right away.

I walked back into the bathroom where Steve was still wiping down Logan's face. The reality of the situation struck me like lightning. There was blood splattered on the mirror, walls, sink, floor, and down the hall were two trails: one from his bedroom, and one to the kitchen. I walked into his bedroom and saw the small pool of blood in his bed. The entire brevity of it was like a crime scene. *Oh my gosh! Oh, sweet baby!* I was startled as my cell phone rang. I did a "hopscotch" past the blood trail back to the kitchen so I could answer. "Hello? Hello?" I stepped outside on the back patio to get a better signal.

"This is Dr. Fearon, returning your call."

"Dr. Fearon, we just awoke to Logan bleeding everywhere. We think it's coming from his nose or mouth, but can't tell."

"Sometimes kids can develop a clot or scab that might break loose, causing a big nose bleed…"

"Wait." I cut off Dr. Fearon as Steve swung open the patio door, putting both hands on the sides of his head as if he was trying to keep it from coming off his shoulders.

Steve blurted, "He's still bleeding…I can't get the bleeding to stop and it's *gushing* now!"

"Oh my gosh. My husband said he can't get the bleeding to stop," I repeated to the silent surgeon on the other end of the line.

His calm voice replied, "You need to take him to the emergency room now to be evaluated."

"Okay, bye." I think I said.

Landon was just awakening, but still in his room.

"We need to get him to the ER. I'll call mom to come over and stay with Landon."

We sat Logan on on the couch in the playroom. I looked over and Steve opened the front door and yelled at our neighbor friend. Lanham was taking out his garbage to the curb when Steve motioned for him to come over. Heather was in her jeep with her kids getting ready to leave to go to our campus we worked at together. Lanham ran over to our house. Our husbands have one thing in common, and it's *not* having a sense of urgency to them. But this time, there was no time to waste.

I made a call to my mom. "Mom, I know it's early, but I need you to come over now, like *right now!*" I can't explain everything, but we have to get Logan to the emergency room.

"Okay, I'll be there shortly," she replied without hesitation. My parents lived about fifteen minutes away, thankfully.

Lanham stepped into the house. "Can you stay with Landon until Lisa's mom gets here? We have to rush Logan to the ER, he's bleeding out."

"Of course," he replied. A few moments later, Heather walked in. I was trying to wipe up more blood because at this point Logan was vomiting blood. I've never seen so much in my life.

Heather saw the hysteria in my face and her counseling tactics began to play. "Are you okay to ride to the hospital?"

"No," as flat as I could answer. My capacity had surpassed its limit.

"Where are your keys?" Steve yelled at me.

"I, I think they're in my purse. Heather, will you sit here with Logan for a second, while I go find my keys?" I didn't even wait for her to answer.

I dug and dug through the mess in my purse until I finally found my keys. "Here they are."

Steve grabbed them and said, "let's go, I've already got pillows and blankets in the back."

"How is Logan getting to the car?" Heather asked.

"He can walk, just help him walk." Steve walked to the garage to start the car.

Walk, I thought? What was he thinking?

Heather began walking behind him with her hand on his back as if to guide him, and then down to the floor, he went onto his knees in a "w" form.

"Oh my gosh." I ran over and sat down on the floor beside him and leaned him in my arms, as if I were going to pick him up, one arm under his neck, and my other arm under his legs. He was passed out cold. I tried lifting him...*I can't lift him, someone, Oh God, please help me! I couldn't speak. Fight or flight snatched my tongue.*

"LANHAM!" Heather yelled to her husband and he rushed over, scooped up Logan's limp body in his arms.

Steve was already on the driver's side with the car running. I got into the back first, set up a pillow, then Lanham placed Logan laying in my arms. Heather climbed into the back with me and slid one arm around me, and one arm on Logan's leg. At this point, he woke up slightly.

Steve peeled out of our driveway, down the country roads. We passed my mom on the way, and I could see she was still in her nightgown and curlers in her hair. I wanted to cry. *No, no... not yet, keep it together. For Pete's sake Lisa, don't fall apart yet.*

Steve was driving in a panic, speeding, honking, and yelling at anyone who got in the way.

Under normal circumstances, I would have picked a fight and told him to quit driving like a maniac before he got all of us killed. But, under normal circumstances, he wouldn't have been driving like this lunatic I saw behind the wheel right now. I knew we were under pressure to get to the hospital, but I didn't want to wreck in the meantime. We lived too far out in the country to wait for an ambulance to come to our house.

In a calm voice, I said, "put on the hazard lights, maybe people will get out of our way. And please don't forget we aren't buckled back here." He turned on the hazards without saying anything to me. I looked down and my right hand was clutching the pillow so tightly my knuckles were white.

We finally pulled into the hospital entrance, and Steve whipped around to the drive at the ER that the ambulances used. He threw the gear into park, and came around and opened our back door as a nurse ran outside with a wheelchair.

I could tell by the wide eyes of the nurse, she was wondering *what the heck?* As they helped him into the wheelchair, we all quick-stepped into the ER, straight to a bed.

My mouth began spewing his medical history, what we found this morning, and where his craniofacial team was. Logan started vomiting more blood. The nurse was trying to get an I.V. started but couldn't. He apologized after he stuck him four times and collapsed a vein later. He said he usually gets it the first time. But, Logan was so dehydrated his veins wouldn't allow it.

The ER physician arranged for us to be transported by ambulance to Medical City Dallas Hospital where his team was and paged Dr. Fearon, letting him know we would be arriving today. He said the paramedic would be bringing in the gurney soon.

It was just Logan, Heather, and Steve and I in the room. Logan laid his head back and drifted in and out of consciousness. I whispered to Logan to try to stay awake. I think I was afraid if he fell asleep or unconscious that he might not ever wake up again.

I looked over at Steve who sat down on the other gurney that was horizontally against the wall, dropped his head, and clenched the mattress with both hands until the sheet was taught.

I looked at Heather, who, bless her heart was trying to keep some sort of positive vibe for us. She gave me a fake "cheese" smile. Our eyes spoke.

I walked over and sat down next to Steve, and slid my arm around him while Heather pulled the curtain in front of us to give a moment of privacy.

"This is just a bump in the road. We're gonna get through this. God is going to take care of Logan, keep praying." It felt good to actually say this out loud because I needed reassurance too.

The door opened and the paramedics came in and transferred Logan to their ambulance gurney.

"I hear they weren't able to start an I.V., but to give you assurance, we will keep a very close eye on his blood pressure. It looks a little low right now, but nothing too dangerous. If need be, we do have a way of intravenous through bone, but it's the last resort. I'm telling you this so you know we do have a way of getting fluids to him if need be."

Oh, Lord. Please don't let him crash on the way to the hospital and need a "bone" I.V. I don't think I can handle anything else.

"Steve, I'll ride with Logan in the ambulance, you meet us over there." I turned to Heather, "will you please ride with him? I don't want him driving alone."

"Of course," she replied.

I hopped into the ambulance and sat on the designated seat.

Steve though, had another ride coming.

****

Steve's Ride

Steve and Heather got in my SUV to follow us to the hospital, and my low fuel light dinged. Steve laughed, an awkward, "are you kidding me?" kind of laugh. It was surreal that they had to stop and do something so mundane, but necessary, while Logan was in an ambulance being rushed to the hospital.

He drove to the gas station and filled up. Before they took off for the hospital, Steve dialed his Dad on his cell phone.

Steve couldn't speak. He put his head into the steering wheel, began to cry, and without a word, handed the phone to Heather.

"This is Heather. There's been an emergency and Logan is in an ambulance headed to the hospital in Dallas. I'm in the car with Steve, and we are on our way there now. He wanted to let you know."

Alarmed, Steve's dad wailed, "What happened?

"Logan is okay, but it's serious," Heather replied.

"We're headed that way," Steve's dad replied. He raised his voice to Steve's mom as he was hanging up the phone, "Call the church! Tell them to start praying. We need to get to the hospital now."

****

Ambulance Ride

The paramedic asked me questions to get all of his medical information and kept me updated on his vitals. He was stable and resting.

I texted Heather since I knew Steve was driving and gave her an update to share with Steve. I hoped this would give him a little peace.

When we arrived at the ER, the nurse got an I.V. started on the first try. He cried. He hates needles, I.V.s, blood work, shots...but can you blame him? I was so relieved she was able to get one in him. It reassured me they could give him what he needed, and quickly, as far as fluids or medications. By this point, his bleeding had stopped.

After a CT scan and blood work, the results showed nothing.

"Dr. Fearon is in surgery right now, but he has been paged to stop by and assess his situation," the ER physician explained. "We will keep an eye on him in the meantime."

Around 2 p.m., Dr. Fearon came by to check on Logan. By this time, he seemed fine and back to normal.

"Tell me about this nose bleed."

I explained everything that happened this morning.

He took his flashlight and looked up into his nose, mouth, and ears.

"I'm not seeing anything unusual, or what might be the cause of the nose bleed," he said a little puzzled. "I checked his blood count from the chart, and it is a 7, so he doesn't need a blood transfusion. It could be that there was an internal scab that broke loose, and gave him the world's worst nose bleed."

"Well, I guess that's good news. So what now?" I asked.

"His vitals are good, so I will sign the discharge papers. Go home and take it easy, and call me if anything comes up, or he has any more problems."

****

Over the next week, I didn't sleep. I would get up in the night, multiple times, to check on Logan. I was so afraid it was going to happen again. An uneasy feeling of dissatisfaction from the prognosis we were given left me anxious, but I couldn't explain why. I went into his room at night while he was asleep, took the pen-shaped flashlight I confiscated from the hospital, and shined it up in his nose to see if there was any more bleeding. But, I didn't see anything.

However, one of the nights I went into his bedroom with my handy flashlight, Logan was sleeping with his mouth open. I noticed in the very back of his pallet, there was a small hole about the size of a pencil eraser. I had never noticed it before, so my plan was to call the doctor the next day to find out if he needed to be seen about it.

My mom came over the next day to help out and be with us. Steve had gone back to working nights the day after the incident and had been asleep for about two hours. Since she was there to help, I told her I was going to step outside and sit on the front porch swing for a few minutes to decompress. I hadn't been sitting outside five minutes, and I heard it again. Same tone, same words, same manner.

"Mommy!" Pause. "Mommy!"

I rushed inside and found Logan sitting on the couch. My mom had just fed him some ice cream and was in the kitchen cleaning the bowl.

"What is it bud?"

"It's happening again. My bleeding."

My mom came from around the kitchen bar with a fresh, wet rag. "It must have just started."

I saw red liquid spilling from his nose again. My stomach turned.

The true test was revealed.

****

"Steve! Steve! We have to go. It's happening again. Logan is bleeding again, so we need to go straight to Medical City Dallas."

Steve bolted up, stared at me with his sleep-deprived expression, then jumped up, and started getting dressed.

I quickly grabbed the rescue tools for his halo, my purse, and some plastic bags in case he started vomiting, and Logan's puppy. We were out the door within minutes. I sat in the back with Logan resting on my shoulder. I could tell he was becoming lethargic again. I called the hospital's emergency room, letting them know the situation, that we were there a week prior, and we were on our way.

When we arrived, Steve carried him inside and after we checked in, we sat in the waiting room, but only for about five minutes. Steve laid him on the bed, and the ER physician came in and started asking us questions. Logan started vomiting blood again. The doctor asked us how long he had been doing this, and with a quick, but long-winded reply, I spilled everything that had happened the prior week, in about thirty seconds.

"Okay, the nurse will start an I.V. and we will check his blood levels."

Within about fifteen minutes, the doctor came back in to give us the news.

"We need to go ahead and admit Logan to a room and start a blood transfusion. His blood levels were a 5, which is much lower than they should be for his age. I've paged Dr. Fearon, so he knows you all are here and will make a visit tomorrow morning to check on you. The nurses will take good care of him."

"Okay, thank you." I was partly alarmed, but partly relieved that at least he will be *admitted,* this time, giving us peace of mind if something happens, we were right where we needed to be: in the hospital with all the healthcare providers!

The next morning, Dr. Fearon came by and said he put in orders for the ENT to take a look into his nose. We headed to the fourth floor in building B. The doctor took us back into a room and pulled out a long scope with a light on the end. *Oh, come on. I can't even. There is no way Logan is going to let this doctor stick that up through his nose.*

Logan squirmed and hollered and cried, all the while Steve and I tried to talk him through it. Unsuccessful, the doctor gave up, thank goodness. I could tell he felt bad for Logan and didn't want to make him more uncomfortable than he already was. *Well, that appointment went over like putting socks on a rooster.* The doctor prescribed a nasal spray as a vasoconstrictor hopefully to stop any future bleeding.

Back to the regular room we went. The nurses came in and out, checking on him and giving him more nose spray, which he hated because the spray would come out through the hole in his pallet. Dr. Fearon said that the hole was a fistula and wasn't the source of the bleeding, but *would* need to be fixed. However, it would need to wait for a future date and time since we had more urgent matters right now. We were hoping perhaps this nose spray would constrict enough, allowing whatever the issue was, heal.

About eight-thirty p.m., it was a little after the nurses shift change. I was by his bedside when the trauma started all over again. Logan started bleeding and vomiting blood again. It caught me off guard. Every bit of color drained from his face until he was pale and almost gray. One of us hit the nurse button and called for urgent help. The nurse swiftly came into the room, and panic swept across her face. Blood was everywhere. I babbled something through my hysteria, and Steve was getting some towels from the bathroom.

The bleeding subsided after our repetitive efforts of pressure, then the three of us took Logan to the bathtub with warm water to try and get him cleaned up. The nurse had to call for a cleaning service to come and change bedding and mop the floor. After everything was cleaned up, she walked over to the bathroom and asked if we were doing okay, or if we needed anything. I was in a squat position to help support Logan in the bathtub, and Steve was to his left helping him get cleaned. Bless her heart.

All my grace flew out the window as I yelled, "Why does this keep happening? I don't understand! This is not okay! He's losing so much blood!" I fell down from my squat onto the cold, hard bathroom floor and looked at the nurse. Hot tears streaked my face as I then said calmly, "I'm sorry. I'm not upset with you. It's not you. I can't take seeing this happen anymore. Why don't we have answers?"

In her sincere reply, she said, "I am so, so sorry this is happening. I've paged the doctor, and hopefully, he will be calling back soon."

After the doctor replied, he ordered another draw to check his blood levels. Within about thirty minutes, the nurse came back with another pint of blood and said his levels were low again, so he needed a second transfusion. It was a long night.

****

The next morning, Dr. Fearon came by the room. He felt like the issue had to be somewhere in his nasal cavity, but without being able to see up there, it was hard to tell. So, after much discussion, the decision was for Logan to go into the ER for a sedated exploration of the nasal cavity with the ENT as well as the Gastroenterologist to check his stomach. This was scheduled for late afternoon, which meant no food for Logan.

They wheeled him off to the OR, and Steve and I waited in the waiting room. Heather had called me earlier in the day and asked if we needed anything from the house. I asked her to take care of our dog, Snoopy, and to bring Steve and me a change of clothes.

She met us in the OR waiting room with a sack of our things and sat with us for a moment. She looked at us both and said, "Oh, you both are so pale. I know you're under a lot of stress, but if you can take turns, try to go outside and let the sun hit your face. Do it for yourselves." We hugged and I thanked her for driving all the way to bring us things.

I guess it's really true, the way fear in someone's face is described in books: *the blood drained from her face like she had seen a ghost.*

About an hour later, the doctors met us in the waiting room, practically scratching their heads. Nothing, except that his stomach looked great, so there was no issue there. To our dismay, the ENT couldn't find anything in his nasal cavity to show any injury or source of the bleeding. It was disheartening to hear.

Dr. Fearon said he would keep researching and brainstorming until we figured this out. Until then, we stayed another night at the hospital. I prayed every day and every night.

I took a walk and went downstairs. I went outside into a small private outdoor atrium with a few trees, lovely landscaping and a few benches. The sun was shining. It felt strange to me, because inside the hospital it's hard to decipher day from night at times. It was so peaceful outside except it contradicted every internal feeling I had. I wanted to scream. *Could anyone possibly know what it's like to watch your child suffer over and over and over? Are there others out there that feel the pain that we do right now?* I was mad at the world, and I'm not sure why because the world didn't do anything to me. I needed an outlet. I closed my eyes and let the sun hit my face. I breathed the fresh air. After a few more minutes, I made my way back to the room.

****

A few days later, he approached us with conviction that the source had to be somewhere in the nasal or sinus cavity, and most likely much farther than they probed during the first exploration. He proposed going back to the OR with the ENT for a second time, to probe further to see what they find. He said they would make sure to have blood ordered and ready if he needed it. Steve and I agreed to it. Logan's life depended on it.

Within an hour, Dr. Fearon came out and said they found the culprit. Way up in Logan's cheek was a tear in his artery that kept pooling and bursting, causing an aneurysm.

I couldn't believe what I was hearing. He was bleeding out with every incident. How is he even still here?

Dr. Fearon continued with his explanation, "For tonight, the ENT has packed Logan's nose with saline-filled balloons, to keep the bleeding under control. I've called the IR physician (Interventional Radiology) who will come visit with you in the morning, and perform a procedure to clamp the artery to stop the bleeding. He will give you more details and answer any questions you have about it. So for now, you guys try to get some sleep."

Answers. We finally had answers after almost two weeks in the hospital. We've spent more time in the hospital for this go-round, than his scheduled surgery. Relief embraced me. The unknown is unbelievably frightening and drains the ever-loving life out of you. *One more procedure. We need to get him through this one more procedure, then, he will finally be on the road to recovery.*

The next morning, Logan went back into the OR for the third time, but this time, there was a remedy to the problem. It didn't take very long, but it warranted a night's stay in the ICU because he needed yet a third blood transfusion.

"Steve, if you want to try to get some rest, go down the road and get a hotel room. I'll stay in the ICU with Logan. Neither of us has slept for days."

"Nah, I'll just go down to the big surgery waiting area and see if I can find a couch. I don't want to be too far away if something happens."

Unfortunately, there were only a few couches, and they were already taken. Steve sat on the floor and leaned up against the wall and tried to sleep.

****

It was a rough night, for everyone, but we made it through once again. The next morning, they moved us back to a regular room. After a few days of recovery, our families came to visit. Logan's blood count was finally healthy, and he didn't need any more transfusions. Logan has always been a long and lean kid, but he was so thin and frail from losing so much weight during this ordeal. Our next challenge was to help him gain his strength back and some of the weight he had lost since his halo device would still be attached for three more weeks. After all of this suffering, we wanted to take our boy home ("…Weeping may tarry for the night, but joy comes with the morning." ~ Psalm 30:5).

After two weeks, three blood transfusions, hundreds of tears, and countless prayers, we got our golden ticket home.

****

Logan received a letter in the mail from his great, great, Aunt Virginia (Ginna – the one who wrote the poem). I opened the envelope and read aloud her words written in cursive:

6/24/11

Dear Logan,

I've been waiting for your address because I wanted to write you a letter. Then, after your Aunt Cherrill sent it to me, I got a sore in my nose (very painful, from oxygen). A week later, I had a painful fever blister, and this week a very painful lump on the inside corner of my nose and eye. I had to go to the doctor and get medicine for infection. This little bit of hurt doesn't compare to what you've been through. I got scared and cried, didn't want to go to the doctor. I was praying for you all the time and reminded myself of how brave you are and got ashamed of myself. I decided to be like you…BRAVE!

Now I'm on the mend and want to thank you for inspiring me to be quiet and depend on God to take care of me.

I saw two cute little boys on TV yesterday. They were playing in older boy's home; they were 9 & 10. The ten-year-old was playing the piano and the other boy was laying on the sofa eating gumdrops. He put too many in his mouth and got choked; couldn't breathe. The older boy knew what to do. After three attempts to get the candy out of his throat, he gave the little boy a hard treatment and save his life. Each of these boys had been taught by nurses – their mothers.

Your sweet mother can explain this to you, if she can read my writing. I'm too slow at printing. I thought you'd enjoy this story. The fire department gave him a trophy for saving a life.

I've wanted to write you another poem and will keep trying, but can't seem to get started; not enough information. But, I know you've been through a lot and I'm always praying for you and your family.

Love, Love, Love
God Bless you
Your old, great, great Aunt Ginna

This was a treasure to receive after the ordeal we'd been through over the last few weeks.

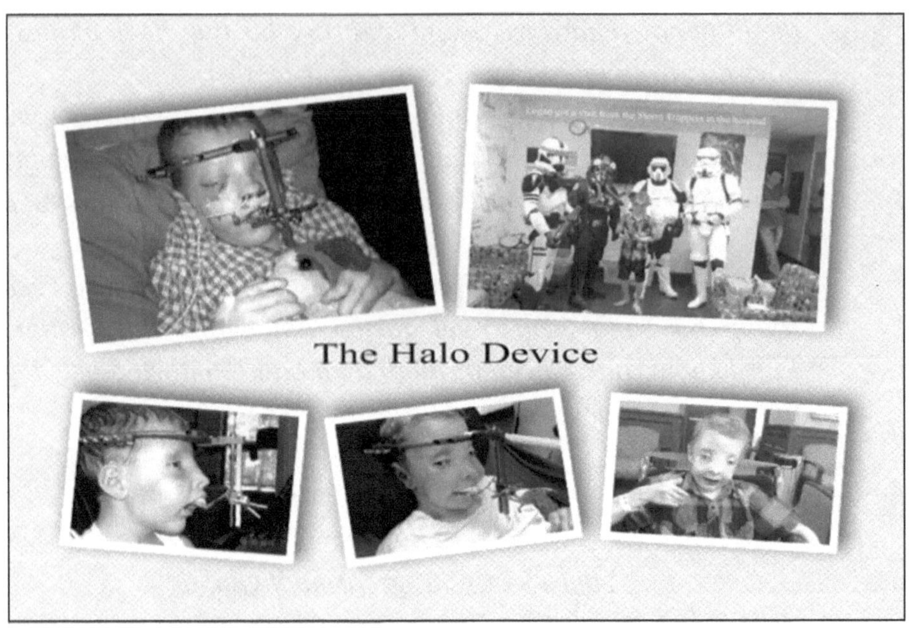

The Halo Device

Before & After Midface Advancement

Chapter 18
Independence Day - Freedom Has New Meaning

"...in me you may have peace. In the world you will have tribulation. But take heart, I have overcome the world."
~ John 16:33 (ESV)

On July 1, 2011, Logan went back into surgery to finally have the halo removed. This was a piece of cake, relatively speaking. He didn't even have to stay in the hospital overnight! This surgery took about thirty minutes. They monitored him for a couple of hours to make sure he was drinking and eating, long enough to confirm he was holding it all down and the anesthesia wore off. They did one final x-ray to review his skull structure and make sure the bone filled in. The verdict: all good.

Finally, it was over. He was breathing well, his eyes were now protected, he could smell, taste, and chew better. He was still trying to regain his strength and weight back. Since it was so close to the fourth of July, I wanted to have a celebration at our house with family, friends, food, and fun. I mean, what better way to celebrate the removal of the halo? Talk about freedom.

We hosted the party at our house, and it was another triple-digit day. Luckily, we bought an above ground pool for the kids (and adults) to swim in and cool off. Logan was even able to wear his swimming mask. Exhilaration filled the atmosphere. I had party treats for the kids, and since we were under a burn ban in our county due to the blazing heat, we weren't allowed to shoot off fireworks. So, in turn, I had red, white, and blue balloons filled with helium.

Everyone gathered inside to fill their plates with delicious grub, and I asked if they would all join me in prayer. I wasn't sure if the words would even exit my mouth, nor was I sure of what I was going to say. We bowed our heads, I felt Heather's hand gently placed on my shoulder, and the waterworks started.

The only thing I could do was simply speak what God laid on my heart. I thanked Him for a lot of things and people, but most of all, for blessing us with His presence during our arduous hospital journey.

Although it was the most traumatic experience any of us had ever been through, things could have gone another direction. There were more serious issues that could have arisen. We brought Logan home, when some parents aren't able to.

After everyone ate, we handed out balloons to everyone and had a countdown to release. 3...2...1. All the balloons were released into the air and we watched them float high up into the sky, saying goodbye to the halo while the song "Firework" by Katy Perry played on the radio. It was cathartic. I think this celebration was as much for me as it was for Logan. No mother, father, grandparent, or relative should experience what we had. But, there's freedom in letting go. This was the first step.

****

Around four weeks after the halo removal, I was in the kitchen milling around. He still had some swelling that hadn't subsided yet. I heard him call me.

"Mommy."

Only to my surprise when I turned around, it was another little boy standing there. It *was* my boy, only with his *new* face. I loved his new face with every ounce of my being, but frankly, it took some getting used to, for all of us. Mainly because it dealt with change, and change is hard.

We also had to adjust to life, and let life get back to "our normal." To say the least, this was the most impactful change in our lives.

Over time, I realized I was grieving. I didn't lose my son and no one passed away. I grieved the loss of the face I once knew. He is still the same strong-spirited boy who endears my heart, whom I still learn from every day. I will always admire his strength to overcome the obstacles life has thrown at him. Through it all, he came out a champion. I watched him in awe with his triumphant tenacity. I've learned what it means to have real grit.

What puzzled me now was how to deal with sadness and celebration all at the same time.

How am I supposed to feel? If I am sad about him looking different from his previous face, I feel guilty. If I am happy about him looking different with his new face, I feel guilty. I was at war with myself. How do I deal with these emotions? How will he deal with these emotions? Will he like his new face?

The *doozy* spared no anxiety. I have adjusted to the new, but not forgotten the old. I still miss that face from time to time, especially when I see his pictures from past years. But as I watch him now, laughing and talking about his day along with all his quirky stories, it is well with my soul.

****

Over the next two years, we enjoyed doing fun things. Six weeks after the halo removal, my mom and I flew to Wyoming with the boys to my sister's house. This was their first time flying in an airplane, and they did great.

I deeply needed this time with my sister to decompress, feel normal, happy, safe, and be silly like we always are when we're together. Her two children are the same age as my boys, give or take a few months, so they always have so much fun getting together as cousins.

She drove us to Rapid City, South Dakota where we visited Mount Rushmore. Then we drove over to see Devil's Tower, the famous mountain that the actor made from a pile of mashed potatoes in *Close Encounters of the Third Kind*. The sightseeing was all pretty spectacular. The normalcy allowed us to breathe.

Back home, after everything settled, raw emotions surfaced and mandated conversations and counseling. At one point, Logan told me he thought he was ugly. I was heartbroken. Like any mother, I assured him he was not ugly, but that he was a smart and handsome boy. He didn't like that even after his halo surgery, people still stare. He even told the school counselor he wished he could be king of the world so he could make it illegal for people to stare.

These were some hard times, but with family, counseling, faith, and friends, we stood by him and helped him through.

****

In 2013, Logan underwent another anterior (frontal) cranial vault. He had been having headaches and some strange sensations he described as "little things crawling around on my brain."

Funny, how this surgery was so second nature that we didn't flinch when we got this news. He was 11, about to be 12 years old for this one, and right before Christmas.

His sixth grade class even signed a poster that had a digital picture printed of Captain America with a photo of Logan's face digitally pasted onto it, holding his shield. They wrote words of encouragement and sweet sentiments like: "keep calm and be awesome;" "You are one of the strongest and bravest people I know;" "I'm praying for you;" "Get well soon buddy;" "Logan you are a super hero;" "Stay strong and get well;" "I will be praying for you, and we will see you sometime in January."

My sister was able to come into town for this one. It was so nice just having her sit next to me.

Once again, we found ourselves in the surgery waiting room at the hospital. Both Steve's and my parents were there, as well as Donnie and Karen Foster, our pastor and his wife. The support of our loved ones surrounded us with warmth and comfort. However, for some reason, I felt uneasy, a strange feeling I hadn't felt before. I worried, is this a sign? Are we going to lose him in this surgery? What is this feeling? We've been through this so many times. Perhaps it was more of a…*stirring.*

After approximately five hours, we got the call from the surgical nurse.

"They're all finished. He is doing fine and will be moved to the PICU now. Head up to the third floor to the PICU waiting room, and the doctors will talk to you both soon."

I put aside my apprehension, and we all gathered our things and took the elevator to the third floor. We're getting really good at this waiting game.

About twenty minutes later, Dr. Fearon came out and gave us the news we wanted to hear.

"He's doing great! He did have a few tears in his dura, but I stitched those up and we flushed him with a lot of antibiotics, so he should be covered. He has plenty of room now for growth. The nurses are getting him settled now and will come out to get you in a little bit."

Steve and I thanked him and I hugged the doctor once again. I sat down on the chair next to my sister and she turned to me and asked, "Do you get butterflies in your stomach when you see the doctor after surgeries? When he came out of those doors and walked toward us I immediately got butterflies in my stomach…how do you do this all the time?"

"I used to get butterflies all the time, but now it's more of an anxious feeling…like I want him to hurry up and come out, with good news of course, so we can get this healing show on the road," I said with a crescent smile.

****

Luckily for Logan, and us, he was allowed to make visits to the coveted teen room in the hospital, which housed a pool table, video games, music, etc., once he was moved to a regular room after a couple of days. His favorite though, was the mobile Wii station they wheeled into his room at each of his requests.

This was a turning point for me. Something stirred inside me as I processed my worries I encountered while we were waiting during his surgery. I felt it was time to start writing down bits and pieces of our experiences as a "craniofacial family" to share with others. I believe God lay this on my heart to share, so others could connect too, and not feel so alone. So, I started a blog titled One Real Hero. I sat down at the computer one night after I tucked the kids in bed, and began typing my first blog. It was mainly an introduction to our family, who we were, what state we lived in, and how our story all started. I added a few pictures of our family, the boys, and one of Logan with our dog Snoopy.

I spent a good two hours fretting over the themes, colors and styles of my blog. I was so nervous about posting it, but knew I had to buckle down and do it. It's hard being transparent and allowing vulnerability to come to the surface. Over the years, I have placed stock into what others think of me…too much so.

I got everything set up, and stared at the keyboard. Push the button. Click post. Do it. I pushed the button. I did it. I felt I had taken off all of my clothes in front of the world. Then, I learned only people who subscribed to my blog would see it. Oh, okay. I see how it works now. The whole world didn't see it after all.

For family and friends to follow, I created a social media page called One Real Hero as a platform to share my blogs. I mustered the courage and sent out a post on my personal Facebook account for people to learn more about our story by following the page.

And there you have it. There's no turning back now. We're exposed. But, from all of our experiences so far, I wanted to connect with people. There were friends and family who wanted to keep up with how Logan and our family was doing, so this was an easy way to give updates.

I was also ready to meet other Apert families. I craved it. I needed Steve and I to connect with others. I was prepared to get off this secluded little island I felt we were on, and hear stories, meet families who were on the front line like us. I needed to know that we weren't alone. I also hoped Landon would see there were other kids who had siblings like his. I wanted Logan to know he wasn't the only one.

Chapter 19
Time to Meet Some People Like Us

*"You keep a lot to yourself because it's difficult
to find people who understand."*

~ Unknown

2014

I joined a Facebook group called Apert International, started by a wonderful mom and dad, Don and Cathie Sears, with a daughter who also had Apert Syndrome. When I found it, I immediately befriended moms and dads who had children with Apert Syndrome. There were more families as well I connected with whose child had different craniofacial diagnoses. It was heartwarming, and I immediately began to feel a sense of belonging. I showed Steve and the boys pictures of other families and their children.

I came across a mom who I found out lived in Dallas. *No way.* I sent her a friend request on Facebook. We connected right away. She asked me if we had ever been to the yearly family retreats with the Children's Craniofacial Association, to which I replied we had not. We had had so many surgeries, year after year, or Steve working out of state, or moving into a new house, or more surgeries, that we never had the time or the money.

She encouraged me to attend some time. I felt like we were finally in a relaxed state of mind, and we were ready and open to do this. Well, at least I was. I knew it would be an important feat, so if I had to drag my family there, so be it.

I discussed it with Steve, so we decided to attend our first retreat in 2014, held in St. Louis, Missouri.

We had three days of meeting families, children, and adults, all of whom were affected by a craniofacial condition. For the first time since Logan was born, aside from our own family and personal friends, I felt safe. We were in public but still in the safety zone. Steve and Logan are naturally introverts, so it took them some time to warm up to the situation. As I watched Landon interact with the other children, I could see his sweet, tender heart reaching out to the other children. Seeing that other kids had brothers or sisters with different appearances was a game-changer for him. There was some relief assuring me we have a village...families who understood without judgment.

****

After the retreat, the director emailed me and asked if I would write an article about our experience as first time attendees, to go in their quarterly newsletter, so I obliged. Here is what I wrote:

Reflections

Before I settled back into the daily routine of life, I took some time to reflect on the past five days of an amazing experience - my family's first CCA Retreat in St. Louis, MO. I have seen all the Facebook posts and pictures over the past few years of previous retreats, and have really wanted to go, but for many reasons I have been dragging my feet on planning this trip for my family. Some reasons were the timing of surgeries, Steve's work schedule and being able to take off the time that the retreat was scheduled, but also it was my fear of the unknown. Apprehension seemed to have kept me from choosing to register, mostly because I didn't feel I was ready. I knew that attending a retreat like this might force me to face and relive some emotions all over again and was worried that it might not be what I expected, or wanted from this trip. Who wants to go on vacation with the possibility that it might turn out to be depressing and emotionally draining? Luckily, this retreat was quite the contrary! And now that we have finally gotten the opportunity, and made the choice to be a part of this journey, I feel that my life has been forever changed. So what do I take away from this experience? I take away the sense of acceptance, being part of another family, a much bigger family with delightful people who have "walked the walk", if you will, and have felt the pain of witnessing their child's surgeries and struggles. Even though we didn't necessarily discuss all of our surgeries and experiences with each other – family-to-family, I felt there was an unspoken comprehension of what we've all been through. I thought to myself, "these parents get it.... they have been on the front line, and know what it's like to hear the constant beeping of the hospital monitors, the needles and I.V.s (oh those dreaded needles!), pain management, the turning of devices, the tube feedings, the anxiety, sleeping on those awful hospital chairs (or not sleeping at all), the swelling after surgeries, (I know I'm leaving out a lot of medical events here), signing and attending hundreds of IEPs, and advocating for your child on so many levels." This gives me comfort knowing that you truly understand. Although our social media provides great tools for connecting with others now, there's something to be said about face-to-face interaction, and perhaps this is what makes it so surreal. As a parent, it was therapeutic to finally connect with people in person who understand where you're coming from, regardless of which craniofacial syndrome or diagnosis your child has, and getting the chance to discuss not only the difficulties our children have faced or will be facing, as well as the ones we as parents face, but also celebrate the obstacles and challenges they have overcome. I take away satisfaction in seeing our kids take ownership with confidence in who they are and where they fit into this world, especially as other children who are "like" them, as well as their siblings, surround each other with kindness. I'm certain that I am not the first parent to point out how empowering the retreats seem to be for our kiddos AND their siblings...to know that they are not alone. When I asked my kids and husband how they felt about the retreat, this was their response: Logan (12 with Apert Syndrome) "I actually just felt like a normal guy around here." Landon (9) "I had so much fun and I made so many new friends!" Steve – "I had a great time getting to meet so many new families. Being able to ask questions and also help by answering questions for others who had younger children was very rewarding." I truly feel that this was a pivotal moment in our lives. Going on vacation is always the highlight of the year, but to take a vacation surrounded by people whom I know I don't have to worry about the stares, or whispers, or what they are thinking, and just being able to really leave it all behind, is the ultimate. To sum it all up, I take away a new sense of belonging; and as a first time retreat parent, now I get it. We do belong! We do have something in common with other families! We do not have to feel like 'that' family who has problems, with 'that' child who has so many difficulties. We are accepted! WE are not alone! Regardless of the miles in-between us, we have made some lifelong friends and I cannot wait until the next retreat when we meet again! Thank you Char, Annie and Jill for your dedication to serving all of the

CCA families, and the many ways that you make a difference in so many lives!

****

While at the retreat, I had conversations with a few other moms about a book that had been published two years prior called "Wonder," by R.J. Palacio. This book was a work of fiction, but it was about a boy with a craniofacial difference who was about to start middle school. Most of them were familiar with it and had already read it. I was explaining to others that I really wanted to somehow make a difference in Logan's school district since he was about to start middle school. I was scared out of my mind for him. The elementary he had attended, also where I taught, for the last seven years was a haven. Everyone knew him, accepted him for who he was. But now, he would start middle school with three other elementary schools and one intermediate school pouring into it with hundreds of *new* kids.

There were a few other moms who were advocating for their son or daughter by speaking engagements and incorporating the book into their district.

The conviction took hold of me by the neck of my shirt and steered me to make a decision. I needed to meet with our school district and propose my idea to fight for this cause. Others could benefit from this, not only Logan. Although I initially had Logan's well being in mind, this was about more than that.

As human beings, we are all filled with curiosity, and with it, humans stare long and hard at what they do not understand, can't explain, or have never seen before. Others may research, investigate, or otherwise seek more knowledge about.

I believe education can change the way we respond to others. It won't change everyone. There will always be cruel people who do not take others' into account, but there are so many who do! They want to know things like: *I wonder what happened to them? Why are their fingers like that? Why does he/she look different? What is it called that they have?*

Once we learn information about the unknown, we can be more understanding, and less afraid or distant with those who are different. If we teach our children, "God made us all physically different and unique," they are more apt to become accepting. So, the next time you encounter someone with physical differences, you become more aware of your response around them. Instead of staring at them with a gaping mouth, you may have empathy and be reminded we are all created in God's eyes, for reason and purpose. You can smile or say hello, and not be afraid anymore, knowing it's okay to be curious, everyone is. But, you don't have to be afraid. You can even reach out to those with physical differences...include them. It's a lonely world out there, especially for our children who want to fit in, have friends, and live a life like everyone else.

This is the message I felt needed to get out there. How can I make this happen? I was already feeling anxious, to the point I couldn't sleep. The very thought of Logan going through school, sitting alone at a school lunch table, almost made me sick to my stomach.

So, I scheduled a meeting with the communications director for our school district to propose an idea. What's the worst that can happen? They could tell me no, or they could receive my proposition, and perhaps we could spark a change in the way people view and treat others with differences. I had to try.

Chapter 20
Conviction of the Heart

*"The most difficult thing is the decision to act.
The rest is merely tenacity."*

~ Amelia Earhart

Raising Awareness - Choosing Kind Campaign

I had a meeting with the communications director and presented my ideas for incorporating the book *Wonder* in our district. We brainstormed and came up with a plan for the school year. Excitement ran through my bloodstream. It was time to use this passion to make a difference.

I published posts on my One Real Hero Blog to begin spreading the word:

**Blog
Tuesday, August 19, 2014
Moment of Truth.... Part 1**

I have to say, first: I am blessed to be a mom of two amazing boys: one who was born with a craniofacial difference (Apert Syndrome), and one who has a servant's heart of gold. Second, I'm lucky to be a teacher in the same school district as both of my boys. I have a strong conviction to spread awareness and acceptance of someone who was born "different" by doing a book study with my students this year on the book Wonder, by R.J. Palacio. I was very fortunate to have the chance to introduce this book to Logan's class last year in sixth grade, and the students seemed to

233

enjoy it and grasp the theme of this story. And the wonderful thing about the message is that it can apply to everyone and I really hope that it carries over with his peers, especially now that he is going into middle school this year. But now, God has really laid this on my heart to help spread awareness; and through this book (and my blog) is where it begins.

So, my moment of truth for this school year, as a teacher is: This is my chance, and I hope and pray that through reading this book, I will not only teach some good reading and comprehension skills but somehow instill a deeper understanding of what it truly means to "Choose Kind." I have made a bulletin board outside of my classroom, and I hope that it intrigues others to want to learn more, and read this book when they see what we post onto our bulletin, or when they see the book in the library or hear others talking about it. If you are reading this blog but are not familiar with the book, and you have children, grandchildren, nieces, and nephews that are in the 3rd or 4th grade, I encourage you to read it to them, let them read it to you, or read it with them. If your children are fifth grade and up, have them read it and tell you about it. There is a wonderful message in this book that teaches us about acceptance, bullying, and making choices that can be life-changing...to many.

Blog
Tuesday, September 30, 2014
Moment of Truth - Part 2

It has begun....
I have been chomping at the bit, waiting patiently to share with you some phenomenal things that are happening in our lives right now. Where do I even begin?

I will start by saying that since last spring, I have had a heavy heart knowing that Logan was finishing up his last year at the school that I teach. This is the school where everybody knows his name, his personality, his learning style, etc. So I guess I began having somewhat of an "empty nest" feeling if you will, that he would be leaving and entering into middle school, where perhaps only about 25% of the students would know him. And truthfully, I was actually happy that he would finally get to attend a different school, as I wanted to be able to let the kite string go. However, being that he is not the "typical" kid who is "just going off to middle school and growing up," but rather a uniquely, God-designed young man who was born with Apert Syndrome, burdened me. Knowing how shy and introverted he is, I feared the worst would happen: kids would stare, point, snicker, whisper, or even make fun of him because he looks different; and I feared he would be isolated, or isolate himself in order to cope with whatever he would be dealing with. This sounds very pessimistic of me, but as a mom, I have to face the reality of it in order to advocate and be proactive for my son. First impressions and initial experiences, especially in school, can make or break the mood for the entire year. This sparked a fire in me. Since I had previously read the book Wonder to Logan's class at the end of the school year, I had an idea. I took my ideas to the communications director who is also head of the anti-bullying projects for my school district and she was very interested. The gist of my ideas was basically to try to mesh a choose kind pledge (a pledge encouraged from the book Wonder) with our anti-bullying month. Since August, we have been working along with the district counselors and curriculum directors, and to say the least, this project has become bigger and better than I ever imagined! Everyone is so supportive, and is really taking this and running with it! I cannot wait until the "Operation Choose Kind" campaign kick-off in October! This will now be a district-wide campaign to spread awareness for kids with craniofacial differences AS WELL as taking a stand against bullying. We will also be raising awareness in the community by doing a coin challenge fundraiser for the Children's Craniofacial Association (CCA), promoting and encouraging all to read the book Wonder, district posters will be hanging on the walls of schools, and to top it off, the 7th-grade Character Education class at the middle school will be doing a book study on Wonder.

What a WONDERful way to start the school year!! **Please** *take a few minutes and view the video from our district initiative: https://youtu.be/5sFHLSb4ubI. We will be showing this to the students, staff, and community...Logan AND Landon are featured! After you watch, please share with anyone and everyone, because this is how we spread awareness!!!! After awareness, follows* **acceptance,** *and this is the ultimate goal...for everyone, isn't it?*

Blog
Wednesday, November 5, 2014
Choose Kind Campaign Coin Drive for CCA was a Success! Let's keep the momentum of "choose kind" going!

WSISD Students Raise More Than $2,800 for Children's Craniofacial Association.

As part of White Settlement ISD's Choose Kind anti-bullying campaign, students raised more than $2,800 for the

Children's Craniofacial Association during a district-wide coin drive in October.

Brewer Middle School seventh-grader Logan Brown, who has a craniofacial diagnosis called Apert Syndrome, inspired WSISD's year-long Choose Kind, an anti-bullying campaign that encourages students, staff, and the community to treat others with respect and kindness.

The Choose Kind initiative stems from the book "Wonder" about a fifth-grader who suffers from a severely deformed face and does his best to be just an ordinary kid with an extraordinary face. Wonder is being used in districts throughout the nation as a way to encourage young readers to share their stories and to introduce the Choose Kind theme.

Blog
Saturday, November 22, 2014
Spreading the Word

About a week ago, I had the honor and privilege to address the high school student body at Ft. Worth Country Day School to help raise awareness and acceptance for those with a craniofacial difference. The students had been required to read the book Wonder, and some of them had researched CCA's website and wanted someone from the Children's Craniofacial Association to come and speak about their organization. They hosted an annual dodgeball fundraiser and wanted to donate funds raised to CCA. Representatives of CCA could not make it in the timeframe they needed, so I was presented with this opportunity. It didn't take a second thought for me to agree to take on this challenge, and put my heart and soul into this speech, and to give them a parent's perspective. I compiled a slide show that included a little history of Logan's diagnosis and several pictures of him over the years, showing how he is just an ordinary kid, loving the same things that other kids do. Within my presentation, I spoke some truths about what it is like for a cranio-kid: surgeries, hospitals, needles, and pain. Although the pictures I showed were of all the happy times of him being an ordinary kid, I pointed out that what they didn't see past all the smiles was the anxiety he has experienced over the years of going to public places, the worry of how many people will point and stare at him this time, or which kid is going to call him a name on the playground at the next fast food restaurant. (True personal experiences - for another blog)

The students were very respectful and attentive, and I couldn't feel more blessed for this divine experience that fell into my lap (not by accident I may add). I believe God puts people, situations, and experiences in our lives to teach and strengthen us so that we are able to follow His plan. I hope God is not finished with me, and I pray that I go where He leads me.

Until the next blog,
God bless,
Lisa

****

Blog
Fear Will Not Be Our Dictator
New Places, New Faces

Summer of 2016 my mom and I had the privilege of taking my boys on a road trip back to Wyoming to visit with my sister and her family. It is always refreshing for us to spend quality time with her and let the kids be with cousins because they are growing up, and before we know it, they will be grown and off to college.

Going to new places wasn't always easy for our family, especially Logan, who was now 14 years old. He was quite the introvert and is very self-conscious of being "noticed." The older he got, the more resistant he became about going places. I get it.... at the tender age of 14, teenagers start seeking independence, and dragging them out of bed before 10 a.m. in the summer is torturous for them. This is also the age of trying to fit in and feel like you belong.

This was where my new worry began a couple years ago, but luckily we had two positive events which helped: attending the Children's Craniofacial Association's family retreat, and launching the district-wide Choose Kind Campaign the year he began middle school to help raise awareness for Apert Syndrome and craniofacial differences. This definitely eased his mind, and ours too. The words he used to describe it: "Now everyone knows, and I don't have to worry about it anymore."

Now, let me preface this next part by saying we, as a family, have always gone places and done things as most families do: shop, eat out, go to baseball games, arcades, movies, etc. The decision was made for our entire family, that we would not be secluded in our house and that our children were going to have great life experiences. I mean, why wouldn't we? (You also need to know he has always been a strong spirited child. This is my loving way of saying he is stubborn, but this will be advantageous for him when he's older). But, while staying at my sister's house, we took the kids to their community recreation center, which had indoor water slides, a lazy river, and such. My boys have been there before with their cousins when they were much younger and thoroughly enjoyed it.

The minute we arrived and got out of the car, Logan said, "I don't want to swim, why are you making me swim?"

I have to be honest. I immediately felt irritated that he was trying to get out of doing this. This seemed to be his theme lately, making excuses for doing anything with our family. It's quite a struggle competing with technology time these days with a teenager. What I wanted to say was: "why are you being difficult? We've been swimming in public lots of times."

It's not like we've never been swimming in public, or even to water parks for that matter. I was perplexed because two weeks prior, he had overcome some fears and decided to go to church camp for the first time, away from home, in another state. He chose to take that leap, especially since his brother was going. He was surrounded with people from our church he felt safe with and trusted.

I explained to him that we were here to spend time with our family, and to enjoy this time with his cousins since we didn't see them very often. Besides, he loves to swim and ride on water slides.

We went inside, paid for the entrance fee, and walked to the pool area. My mom, sister, and I were looking for a spot to sit so we could visit while the kids had fun. We found some chairs and were about to sit down when Logan turned and said something to me. It was kind of loud with this being indoors, and everything was echoing, not to mention he is very soft-spoken.

I asked him to repeat what he said, and his words rang loud and clear even though I could still barely hear him: "a group of people has already stared at me."

We had been there less than ten minutes, and those spoken words punched me right in the gut. So there it is. We are back to this. I now understood his message. He was uncomfortable because we were in another state where, in his mind, he worried that people weren't familiar with kids that look like him. I guess I was naive to think we were passed this and everyone in the world would be able to look past the "physical differences" and move on. But we're not. He's not.

We're so used to going places and doing things locally. I forgot that a completely new environment, and these people may not have ever seen anyone like him before, would trigger his anxiety and feelings of fear.

I really had to pause for a moment and collect my thoughts on what to say. But the truth is, I don't always know what the right thing to say is. I didn't want to dismiss his feelings by saying something to minimize the situation. Yet, at the same time, I also didn't want to feed into his fear with my maternal bleeding heart. So, I tried my best to validate his feelings yet still give him some truth, encouragement, and hopefully, a slight sense of empowerment.

"I'm sorry people have stared at you, that must make you feel uncomfortable. Remember, sometimes people look, but don't stare, simply because they are curious. They may be wondering what happened since your fingers and toes look different. But, if they continue and it becomes an unkind stare, then you can always start out with a smile at them or say hi. If they say mean things to you, then tell them you don't like the way they are treating you and walk away."

I knew for him being such an introvert this was a little unrealistic, but it was the most forgiving thing I could come up with...until my passion rose. My empathetic heart was wrenching, almost a little angry, simply for the fact that my son has to feel this way and deal with this daily.

"But mom, my hands look jacked up."

I refrain from responding with my maternal instinct to say, "but your hands are beautiful," because that is not what a fourteen year old boy wants to hear. However, I know what those "jacked up" hands have been through. I've seen him in four casts from elbows and knees down in length, trying to crawl and pick up things at nine months old. Although I would be speaking my truths, I choose other words.

So I ended it with: "this is a moment where you can make a choice to be brave, hold your chin up high knowing that you are loved and God made you and created you just the way you are (Ephesians 6:13-18). Do the things that make you happy and not let fear control you. Or, miss out on the fun and joyful things in life because you are too afraid."

I'm proud to say he chose to be brave. Just like he had for the last 14 years. And when I saw the smile on his face as he floated past us going down the lazy river, my heart could rest again.

When I look at my son's misshapen, scarred fingers and toes, I see beauty, strength, bravery, and courage. And yes, I am his mom, and moms see the good in their children no matter what. I also know how these scars came to be. But, I know this must be how God looks at us too, as HIS children. Even though we are scarred, we are His children. He loves us and sees the good in all of us, no matter what. He sees us with the utmost and purest love...it's all that matters. He also knows every scar we carry.

Everyone has at least one scar, whether visible or not. Perhaps some are ones you wished you could cover up, or even a physical appearance you are ashamed of. A number of us may have emotional scars that are invisible, and have wounded your heart or made you feel less than worthy. It's incredibly hard to live up to the societal standards these days.

God tells us "know how much you are loved" (Ephesians 5:2). Your scars do not define you, because you are a child of the most high God. God created you with plan and purpose (Jeremiah 29:11). Whatever scar you have, visible or invisible, let it be a reminder of the strength and courage you were given to overcome. Jesus has his own scars to prove it.

Even though this will be something he will have to conquer time after time for the rest of his life, I hope the seed is planted. Hopefully, this seed will help him grow in who he is and want to bloom even if there are weeds around him.

Fear will not be our dictator. This lesson was not only for my son, but also for me.

****

October 2016 - The Other Shoe Finally Dropped

The beginning of high school started out fair. We were worried about many things, but mostly because his school was so big he might not find his classes. He rushed around and found each class, memorized where to go, but not without anxiety, stress, and pain in his joints. That was the new struggle, until the other shoe finally dropped.

After much discussion between Steve and Me, I decided it was time for me to resign from teaching so I could be more available for the boys, especially running them here and there for events and such. This meant that we needed to sell our house. Our financial situation wouldn't allow us to remain where we were without me working.

We moved into a different school district, which made me nervous for both the boys. Landon seemed fine with it, but Logan, not so much.

He was mature enough to understand how high school ran, so we gave him a choice to either start fresh at the new school district as a freshman, or continue with Brewer High School (which had an open enrollment policy), thus leaving me as his chauffer for the next four years. He responded without hesitation.

"I DO NOT want to change school districts. People already know who I am and what I have, and I do not want to have to explain to new people, and have more staring," he responded.

Luckily, Brewer was only about a fifteen-minute drive.

I picked up Logan from school one day and asked my usual question, "how are you?" with which his reply was, "I'm exhausted." This reply wasn't unusual. As I drove around the curves of the parking lot, I felt Logan's left hand touch my arm. As I looked over at him, the left side of his face contorted, then he leaned over and started convulsing, banging his head against the window. He was having a seizure.

"Oh, gosh...Okay Logan. You're gonna be okay, I've got you buddy, I've got you," I said out loud as I pulled over on the driveway of the exit, trying to get out of dismissal traffic. My mind went into warp speed. In a nanosecond, I had processed *not* to try to drive him to the hospital myself because of rush hour traffic; to call 911 since he had never had a seizure before, which worried me that there was something going on inside his brain we didn't know about yet, or he had intracranial pressure; and finally during my call to 911 I managed to spew all of his diagnoses and medical conditions, urging them that this was not *his normal*, so they needed to send someone quick, all the while I am trying to keep his head from banging against the car window by putting my hand between his head and the window. The paramedics arrived within minutes.

While the lead guy was asking me questions in an annoyingly calm manner, the others were checking his vitals and blood sugar. (Please don't judge, I loved the paramedics who helped us, and are grateful for their calmness. In moments like these, as a mother, sometimes we just want to yell at the top of our lungs because we've seen enough heartache for our child). The paramedics did their job perfectly. Their calmness kept me from losing my control and hitting the panic button. Logan was coming out of his episode, but still wasn't cognizant of what had happened.

After much discussion of his Apert Syndrome, we decided to have the ambulance transport him to Medical City Dallas, even though it was a good hour and a half away, and it was rush hour. It was agreed that most likely he would be moved there anyway since he already had his craniofacial team of doctors there. As I followed the ambulance, I made a call to my friend Heather and asked her to pick up Landon at my house. Then I texted Steve with "call me, emergency." I knew it might be a few hours before he called back because he was on a day shift at the time, working as a chief dispatcher, and they're not allowed to have their phones on. I went ahead and left Steve a voicemail, telling him we were on our way to the hospital, but Logan was stable and okay.

He called me back while I was driving, and said he would meet me at the hospital.

We spent two nights there, and after two EEG tests, the neurologists concluded he had some abnormal activity on the right side of his brain where there was some scarred tissue. Most likely it was from a past surgery. He started him on seizure medication right away, and then we were discharged.

It should have been easy from there, but the seizure medication caused major depression for Logan. I heard him say horrifically negative things about himself, which was not like him. I took him back to the neurologist, in which he told us that is a significant side effect of the medication he was taking. He prescribed a new medication, but the kicker was that I had to wean him off of the current medication while introducing the new. It was a complicated process, but I made a chart with all the instructions of how much of what to give and when. Finally, after about four weeks, he was adjusted to his new medication and doing well.

My nurturing heart ached. I finally reached my breaking point. It seemed Logan had so many *things* to deal with in life, but this one did me in. I worried immensely when I took him back to school after the ordeal. Worry fogged my brain with new safety questions. *What if he has a seizure at school? What if kids film it with their phones and mock him? What if he injures himself?*

I had already met with the school nurse and administrators to add this to his *plan.* We discussed protocol for seizures, and I left, leaving them with his rescue medication.

I drove the entire way home after dropping him off at school the first day back praying. I asked for protection for Logan, wisdom for any upcoming medical decisions we might make, and most of all strength.

As I drove back home from dropping Logan off at school, my cell phone rang as I pulled into the parking lot of Walgreen's.

It was Logan's school Occupational Therapist, who was also my coworker and friend.

"Hey Lisa, it's Andrea and was wondering if you have a few minutes to discuss Logan's I.E.P since we have is ARD meeting coming up."

"Sure," I replied.

"You know that Logan is doing fantastic, since we talk often. But first I want to ask, friend, how are *you* doing with this new seizure diagnosis?"

I couldn't hold it in anymore. Lucky her, but she had no idea what she was about to receive. My capacity exploded, and the dam broke.

"This is so hard! It's hard seeing him go through this depression. I'm so heartbroken." I sobbed, a hard, ugly cry making me gasp through each breath while she listened and empathized. I wondered *what more will this kid have to endure? Hasn't it been enough?*

After our conversation ended, I sat there in Walgreen's parking lot for another ten minutes, collecting myself. I picked up prescriptions (I remembered this was why I was there to begin with) and drove home.

All the way home, I laid everything down at Jesus' feet, confessing I could not bear the weight of this burden, and even though my heart was broken, I trusted Him and knew He would get us through another trial.

Hopefully, that was the last shoe to drop.

****

November 2017

Three years passed since the "Choose Kind" movement, and we received word that they had made the book *Wonder* into a movie. We were invited by CCA to the premier red carpet event in Dallas. We met two of the actors from the movie and had our picture made with them. It was a memorable event.

Logan was now a sophomore in high school, and the district continued on with the Choose Kind campaign by hosting a movie night for the community's families, so we got to see it twice. They reserved two theater rooms and it was a sell-out.

****

High school boded an arduous journey for Logan. During the teenage years, kids begin finding out their interests and skills, whether it be sports, art, band, agriculture, etc. Inevitably, kids drift apart, find new friends, or their own niche.

Logan dabbled into a little of every elective, with the exception of sports. He participated in the band until his sophomore year, until he realized he didn't have the stamina. Marching band is extremely intense with practice in the wee hours of the morning, during school, and after school. He expressed that he didn't want to participate in the marching band anymore.

Next, he took some agriculture classes, like vet medicine and welding. However, those didn't interest him. What Logan really wanted was automotive classes, but unfortunately, our district didn't provide these classes. His passion is anything and everything about cars, especially exotic ones.

Nonetheless, the next few years made for some lonely lunches during his high school years. He didn't sit alone every single day, but most days he did. He had anxiety every day and was ready to graduate. It hurt. Luckily, we had some pretty awesome youth leaders from our church who came up to school from time to time and had lunch with him. A few times a family member visited to sit with him at lunch. I even left work early one day to go eat lunch with him. After sitting in that high school cafeteria, I quickly understood why he had so much anxiety. The words and conversations I overheard appalled me. There was no bullying, and these conversations weren't about Logan. I heard things I hadn't even heard until way up into my adult years. Inappropriate things. It's sad how desensitized our society has become.

The next couple of years, he was on the home stretch. Steve and I tried to encourage Logan the best we could, reminding him the light is now shining in the tunnel.

Chapter 21
Graduation 2020

~ Anonymous

Our *original* plan for a family vacation and graduation gift to Logan was a cruise from Miami, Florida, on the Carnival Sensation. We had three islands to visit.

First stop was Grand Turk with an early morning excursion, taking a catamaran to a location for snorkeling. There would be a plethora of conch shells to collect, and the guide would set up on the island he took us to and make us a conch salad cuisine. Afterward we would take our souvenir shells back to the ship and set sail again in the evening.

The second stop would have been an island owned by Carnival called Half Moon Cay. Here we would have a full day at the beach, lounging with snacks, drinks, cocktails for the adults, rental water sports, and a yummy lunch at one of the restaurants on the beach.

The final island stop: Bahamas. We had a full day pass for the Atlantis water park resort of water slides, lazy river, wave pools, shark exhibit, etc. Afterward, we would board the ship and set sail back to Miami.

We had everything booked and paid in full since we had planned everything back in November. I created a countdown chalkboard in our kitchen with a drawing of a cruise ship, island, and palm trees where a dolphin was jumping out of the water, revealing its playfulness.

In February of 2020, the president of the United States forewarned an outbreak of some new virus called *Corona Virus, or COVID-19*. It was spreading like wildfire in China and had made its way to the United States, creating a pandemic. Not only was this virus becoming an international threat, but it was also claiming lives.

In March, we had a discussion of whether or not we should cancel our cruise. President Donald Trump had announced the closure of all borders and ports, at least until this virus calmed down. We honestly thought by June, the spreading of this virus would dissipate.

By the end of March, we made the difficult decision to cancel our cruise. The news of this COVID ran rapidly, creating an unpredictable future. Borders were closed, stores and restaurants closed, all by orders of the government. Everything changed. Quarantine *"shelter in place"* orders were issued. Distance learning provided education from schools, via online. People were instructed to work from home if they could, but for those who still served the public, it was mandatory to wear masks and gloves. Inevitably, the world completely changed in every aspect.

We received word that Logan's graduation might be postponed until some time in July. So, in efforts to resume celebrating with a vacation of sorts, we met with our friends and had a discussion. We decided to wait a little longer because the dates were changing by the week.

We finally received an official notification that graduation would be held at the Texas Motor Speedway on Friday, May 29th. Excellent! We all still hold our original dates of requested time off from work for vacation during the first week of June, so this worked out perfectly.

We met again with our friends and discussed booking a vacation home in Galveston, Texas, on Crystal Beach. Steve, the boys and I had vacationed there two years prior in a beachfront house on the northeastern tip of the Bolivar Peninsula. It was as if we had our own private beach. After showing this property to our friends, Steve checked to make sure our dates would even be available since it was so close to the reservation time. He pulled up the house on his phone and chuckled.

"Is it already booked?" I asked.

"You won't believe this, but the exact time frame we need it is the only week available this whole summer!"

"Oh my gosh! Are you serious?"

"Yep!"

I looked at my friend, whom I call Doc, then she looked at me and said, "It's definitely meant to be. You can't explain that."

Her husband quickly spoke up, "I say we book it right now."

We were all in agreement, so Doc and I pulled out our plastic cards and got it booked.

We told the boys right then, and almost in unison, they said, "We get to go to the beach?"

We told them yes and we would be staying in the same house we stayed in a couple of years ago.

"YES!"

The chatter between the boys began with all the things to do while we were at the beach.

"We can go fishing...let's bring our boogie boards...maybe we can also bring the tent and camp on the beach," their conversations continued.

It was settled. We were going to celebrate this graduation. I prepared by gathering items we needed to take with us and started my packing piles.

About four days later, Steve and I both received an email from the school. The school announced graduation was rescheduled to

Wednesday, June 10th in a different location, which was right smack dab in the middle of our vacation we booked and paid for. The new place was the new Globe Life Field for the Texas Rangers. No games had even been played on it yet.

I was standing in the kitchen and turned to look at Steve. "Did you read the email we just got from school?" I asked.

"Yeah," his voice chagrined.

I sighed heavily. "So what are we supposed to do? This is graduation, but also vacation."

"I don't even know at this point," he replied.

After a day of contemplation, I approached Steve with some possibilities of making the best of both worlds happen.

"I have a thought. I looked online at flights from Houston, which is only about an hour or so from Galveston, to fly into Dallas, and back to Galveston that night. If we did, we would only miss one day of vacation, and we would still make his graduation. I checked, and I have enough points for all of our flights through Southwest Airlines, so it wouldn't cost. The other option is cutting our vacation short and only staying at the beach house for three days instead of six. No matter what we do, something's gotta give. There will be sacrifice one way or another. We could ask Logan what he thought of the options.

"Yeah, I guess ask him what he thinks."

So, I presented the options to him. "Logan, what do you think?" I waited, giving him time to process what was presented to him. "Dad and I just don't want you to regret *not* attending the graduation ceremony. And, you'll get to see the brand new Texas Rangers' Stadium."

He decided he was okay with flying back to town for the one day of graduation, then flying back down to the beach. But, he was adamant about not missing more than one day of vacation.

Plans were finalized, again. Our flights were booked for the day of travel.

A few days later, another email arrived with changed graduation times again, but, this time, the change was by the Texas Rangers Organization. They decided they needed to hold practice in the middle of the day, in between high school graduations.

We were sitting on the couch, and I half-shouted, "OH MY GOSH!" Then I fell over on the couch and did a facepalm with my hand.

"What? Do I even want to know? Steve asked. "Is this going to make me angry?"

"Yes, most likely. Don't even look at your phone, email, or text reminders right now."

I knew if *I* felt this frustrated and angry, he might lose his mind over this new change. I went to the kitchen to prepare dinner.

The synapses in my brain accelerated. *Now what?* There was no way we would make our flight back to the beach now, so the only option was to cancel it. This meant we were back to square one. At this point, it was almost an *all or nothing* situation. I reminded myself: *you've been in tough decision-making situations before…you know what to do.* After dinner, I approached Steve. "Well, are you ready?"

He was calm. "I already know it must be a big change, so lay it on me."

"The time of graduation has changed to 5:00 p.m. instead of 2:00, which means we won't make our flight back to the beach. So, I'll have to cancel our flights. It wasn't the district's decision for the time change, but the Texas Rangers' organization made the decision that they needed to hold practice in between the first district's graduation and ours. The next question is, what do we do now?"

"I have no idea," he sighed.

"We're both upset over this. Let's pray about it and discuss more tomorrow after you have slept from your night shift. We can figure out what God leads us to do."

"Yeah, okay."

The next day, my redundant question loomed as I sat on the couch and all I had to do was look at Steve.

"I'm not sure. I was thinking about it all last night at work. I don't think he really cares about going to graduation. Even after we explained the ceremony and location," he stated matter-of-factly.

"I couldn't agree more. He didn't have the best high school experience and voiced how ready he was to get out of high school and not have to go back," I restated.

"Yeah. It's different for him. He wasn't in any clubs, didn't play sports, tried band for several years, but he didn't like it and certainly didn't have the stamina for it. So, I guess it's not as important to him, which is fine," Steve finished.

"I had to ask myself this question last night: Are we pushing him to attend graduation for him or for *us?*"

We were silent for a moment, but it was loud and clear. I think it is fair to say that we desperately wanted to see him graduate, after all his hard work and what he had been through. We saw this boy come into this world with an arduous journey ahead, with no insight as to what his future would hold, or how long he would be with us. Steve and I were both educators, so we valued what graduation stood for: hard work, determination, completion and success. We both knew though, Logan saw it as something different: hard, demanding, depressing, and lonely. Nonetheless, it still warranted conversation.

"Logan, we have something to tell you."

"Let me guess, graduation changed *again!*" he said.

I explained the situation, and we were back in choosing whether to cut the vacation short, or miss the graduation ceremony altogether.

"Dad and I are leaving the decision completely up to you. It is your choice, and we will make it happen, whatever you choose."

"Can't they just mail it to me?" he asked.

"Yes, they can," I replied.

"Then I don't want to go to graduation. This vacation is more important. Spending time with my family is more important to me, than walking across the baseball field, wearing a mask, and getting a piece of paper."

Well then, I guess it's confirmed. We will not attend graduation. Steve and I had mixed emotions with his decision but respected it completely. He had been through enough, so his happiness superseded our desire for the ceremony.

****

I texted Doc and told her what the final decision was. I also told her I would like to create our own *graduation ceremony* for Logan while we were at the beach, and asked her opinion. She didn't hesitate to offer her help.

I went shopping and bought confetti bombs, balloons, paper cupcake holders, and packed them for the trip along with his cap and gown.

We caravanned down south, on a six-hour road trip to the beach house, making one stop at a grocery store to buy our cold perishable foods.

Time was well spent walking on the beach, playing in the ocean, collecting shells, fishing for the guys, and bicycle riding on the beach.

Wednesday rolled around, so I spent the morning baking cupcakes and brownies, while Doc hung balloons with streamers outside on the deck.

After all baking and decorating was complete, I sat down on the couch with Doc. We both had our laptops, and I planned on writing the speech for the ceremony. Words wouldn't form. It was too personal. I didn't know where to start.

I looked over at Doc, and she was already typing. She knew I needed her help, and my shoulders relaxed. She typed up a quick speech and handed me her laptop.

"Here ya go. Look over this and add to it or make changes as you see fit," she said with her bubbly disposition.

I read through and made only a few edits and texted my pastor to ask him what he thought would be a good bible verse to include. He immediately responded so I added it to the speech. The plan was that we would play the graduation music, then Logan would walk up the stairs to the outdoor deck, and sit down. My friend's husband would read the speech as the proxy administrator, then hand it over for Steve to read the scripture, prayer, and closing. Doc's son monitored my phone while it video streamed live on One Real Hero Facebook page.

It was time for graduation, so Logan dressed up in his cap and gown. I took him outside for rehearsal, while also checking the sound and timing of the music. Everything was ready...it was showtime.

Landon, Steve, and I sat in deck chairs over to the side, and the music began. Logan walked up the stairs to the deck and sat in his designated chair. The music phased out, and Doc's husband began the speech:

> *"Good afternoon and welcome proud parents, family members, and friends.*
>
> *We are here today to celebrate a 2020 graduate of Brewer High School. We are here to celebrate Logan.*
>
> *Logan:*

Most students struggle to balance academic demands with work, personal responsibilities, and social experiences. However, your personal struggles have gone beyond those of most students.

From your start in Kindergarten through your high school years, you were presented with various and difficult challenges, not only in academia but challenges affecting your physical health and well-being. Together with the love and support of your family, you have successfully overcome them all. Your trials have helped shape you into the soft-spoken, strong-spirited young man that you are today: A young man with the strength of character, self-awareness, courage, and perseverance.

And Logan, even though your past struggles and successes have led you to who you are today, they do not define you. They have shaped, strengthened, and prepared you to continue to overcome any obstacle you will meet. God never wastes our pain.

The following poem helps sum it all up from what you have successfully navigated during your first 18 years, including 2020 with the changes and challenges due to "the COVID", to what you will face as you begin your next journey. Consider these words:

LIFE IS A CHALLENGE
Life is a challenge – meet it
Life is a gift – accept it
Life is a sorrow – overcome it
Life is a tragedy – face it
Life is a mystery – unfold it
Life is a song – sing it
Life is an opportunity – take it

Life is a promise – complete it
Life is a struggle – fight it
Life is a goal – achieve it
Life is a journey – complete it
Life is love – love it
Life is an adventure – have fun
Life is a duty – perform it
Life is beauty – admire it
Life is great – make something good of it

Now, we would like our graduate to come forward as we call his name:
LOGAN WADE BROWN
(Logan receives his certificate, shakes hands, stands for a picture, then returns to his seat)
Logan, to confirm your new graduate status, you may move your tassel to the left side.
Would Logan's father, Steve Brown, please come forward for the closing remarks." (Scripture and closing prayer)

Steve began reading.
"This is a reading from Philippians 3:12-14"
"Not that I have already obtained this or am already perfect, but I press on to make it my own because Christ Jesus has made me His own. Brothers, I do not consider that I have made it my own. But one thing I do: forgetting what lies behind and straining forward to what lies ahead, I press on toward the goal for the prize of the upward call of God in Christ Jesus."
"And now if you would bow your heads in a word of prayer.
Gracious and Loving God,
We ask now for your almighty hand to be upon our graduate as he and his family and friends celebrate this grand milestone.

May he find comfort and love from his family's continued embrace and support as he journeys through life.

Bless his life from this day forward with health, goodness, and success.

Enable him:

- to stay true to his dreams for Your greater glory,

- to discern what is right, good, and just, and

- to use his gifts wisely and in service to others.

And during this season of new beginnings, we ask that You make his way clear. We ask that You keep his footsteps firm and remind him that You are always with him.

Empower him to walk into the future with faith, hope, and love guided by your light so that he may use his talents to serve your purpose. Lord, we ask for your continued protection, discernment, and reminders that You are always with him and in control.

Grace be to him, grace be to us all.

We ask all this in your Son's name, Jesus Christ.

Amen."

In the middle of the prayer, Steve paused. I opened my eyes and peeked upward from my bowed head, and noticed he was crying. My throat tightened while my eyes stung until the water flowed. I closed my eyes again, but while I was listening to the prayer, an instant flash of moments played before my eyes. They were memories from his birth to surgeries, hospital stays, crawling, walking, running, playing, learning to ride his bike, school, and all the wonderful and arduous memories...until this present moment.

The prayer ended with our cadence of *Amen*, and the song, "School's Out For Summer," sung by Alice Cooper, jammed on the Bluetooth speaker. Confetti bombs went off, shooting ticker tape into the salty air. Steve and I stood up and walked over to Logan. I hugged him tightly and whispered in his ear "I am so proud of you.

You made it Logan...you did it! I hope you feel proud of yourself. I love you so much."

Steve hugged him next, then we took family photos. I happened to look over at the beach house next door, and they were out on their deck clapping too. It couldn't have been better.

I felt a sense of relief. The fact that he made it through school, especially through his tough high school years gave me more capacity in my lungs. I felt like I could breathe again, and I sensed it in him as well. He seemed so much happier, knowing that *that* part of his life is complete. Now the new life chapter will begin. For him, life was just beginning. Although he did not want to pursue any further education right away, we were okay with that. We knew he needed a break for a little while. His childhood robbed him freedom at times, so it was now time to let him take a step back, and find out what was in store for him in the future. He expressed wanting to get a part time job, and we fully supported him.

Not everyone understands that timelines don't apply to every single person, and that's okay. This is his life, and he doesn't need to be on the *world's* timeline. Our job now is to help him navigate through life to achieve his passions and fulfill the purpose God gave him.

Of course, my new worry for him was loneliness. As a mother, you never want your child to be lonesome. He has immediate family, extended family, and church family, which gives me some peace. I know God has a purpose in this world for Logan, and I can't wait to see what the future holds. For right now, he is happy, which is all that matters. God will let us know when it is time for a change.

Chapter 22
Perspectives

"Shared stories build a relational bridge that Jesus can walk across from your hearts to others."

~ *Rick Warren*

The story of this journey wasn't just mine. The whole family shared in it and now it's time you get to hear from the rest of my family. It has taken a lot of begging, imploring, and pleading to put these pieces of our puzzle together. Imagine trying to get someone you know, who already has difficulty sharing their feelings, to tell you their most intimate thoughts on the most traumatic experiences of their lives. Can you imagine how hard it would be? Well, multiply it by three. Honestly, maybe by two. Landon is my communicator, but for Steve and Logan...well it's not their jam.

These three males who have ridden this train ride with me, sometimes feeling more like a train *wreck*, will share some answers with you to some questions, which, perhaps as an outsider, might wonder. Mind you, I had to give them a list of open-ended questions in order to prompt what I felt you might want to know. Although I am the one providing prose, you are about to read their honest, and transparent feelings. We all perceive, process, explain, and grieve in different ways.

****

STEVE

When Logan was born, I was shocked. I had no idea what was happening. I wondered what was wrong, why he wasn't a typical baby, and if he was going to live. My dreams were for him to be healthy and play sports, but those dreams quickly became a different reality. I was engulfed in worry instead of anticipation for the future.

****

It was tough going through all of the surgeries he had to endure. As a father, I felt my role was to not only be a provider, but a protector, both of which were gravely affected. I was distracted at work by worrying about what would happen next, our finances, how much pain he would be in. It did not bode well for my stress management and it also put a strain on our marriage.

The challenges of making the best decisions for Logan as well as the fears and anxiety provoked us both questioning if we were doing everything right to help him be safe, healthy and lead as normal a life as possible. Lisa and I often had disagreements of how to handle discipline as well. I am the stern one and she is the more lenient one, but I guess that goes for a lot of parents, too. However, it made it harder for us to find the best medium ground. We both had the same goal in mind: to teach him responsibility so that he can grow up to be independent, and push him to his fullest potential.

It took many arguments with our difference in parenting opinions and sleepless nights to come to a point where we had to find some middle ground. Lisa has a strong sense of empathy. While my empathy has strengthened over the years, I have a strong work ethic mentality. So, you could easily say we are like oil and water in that respect. With that said, she also has a better understanding of everything that encompasses special needs. I've had to learn about sensory processing, attention deficit hyperactivity disorder, delayed processing, learning disabilities, and so on.

It forced many uncomfortable discussions about medications, school, and surgeries. These are not typical issues that married couples should have to deal with. They will either make you a stronger couple or tear you completely apart. I think it's safe to say that we have sat on both sides of the teeter throughout this ordeal.

****

When talk of having another child arose, I was apprehensive. I worried we would have problems again with the next one. Since we didn't know much about Logan's diagnosis, I worried that if he passed away, the effect would be devastating not only for us, but for his sibling as well. But, we have learned to pray and put God in the center of all things. Without God, church, and a strong family support, it would have been impossible.

****

Over the years we had so many scares with Logan's health that sometimes I had to go off and cry. Some situations got too much for me to handle, that I walked into an empty hospital room a few times so that I could be alone and cry. I also remember the time when Logan was rushed to the hospital in an ambulance with me following. I had to make the call to my parents and tell them about the bleeding incident, but I couldn't even speak. I handed the phone to our friend Heather so she could explain the situation. I had never felt more afraid in my life that Logan was going to die, and there was nothing I could do to stop it.

****

When I made the decision to change careers and had to move to Wyoming, I didn't think much would change in the beginning. But, it became tough when the house didn't sell, not allowing them to move up here so we could all be together again. I had a few moments where I wondered if the boys would forget me, so I sent them postcards and pictures as often as I could.

There was a disconnect from our friends, due to my job and being away for so long, and it made for an isolated journey.

When I did move back home, it was another adjustment. I had to work different shifts on different days of every week. My stressors didn't disappear, they only changed again. I had to schedule my vacation for surgeries so that I didn't miss work. My *new* biggest fear now was failure. The future was so unclear with having to learn another new job, that all I could do was trust the plan that God had laid out before me.

****

Although I sometimes still struggle with being overwhelmed and stressed, over time, I have learned to lean more on God, rather than my own knowledge. For some reason, I always felt relaxed and at peace during Logan's surgeries. The stress for me came afterward, especially during the times he was in pain and I couldn't make it go away.

I have slowly learned that God is in control, not me. I am more conscientious of other kids with disabilities or medical problems and hope they are okay.

I've become more trusting in God, knowing that He has a plan, even when I don't know what it is, and He will see me through it.

****

LANDON

The most difficult thing I've had to deal with growing up with Logan is his sloppiness. I love him to death, but with my OCD and naturally being a clean person I can't stand it. If you ask either one of my parents they will testify to the countless number of times that I have, and continue to complain about sharing a bathroom with him. I have NEVER had a two-sink bathroom, and since he is older, Logan always gets the big side of the counter. Constantly cleaning the messes made on the counter, wet towels left on the floor, shower mats soaked with more than enough water. Worst of all, the bathroom develops a moldy, humid, almost wet smell. It seems to me impossible to get rid of.

****

Growing up, what was the easiest part about having a sibling with special needs? I have never seen Logan as different. Granted, I haven't had a "normal" brother so it's all I've ever known, is to have a sibling with craniofacial deformities.

****

I feel that when we were younger, Logan did receive more attention. However, it did not bother me. In fact, sometimes I preferred it and wanted his needs to come before mine. In all honesty, I felt like I could take care of myself and knew I would be okay without *extra* attention.

****

Did you feel that Logan got more slack in responsibility than you? If so, how did that make you feel? I definitely believe that 100%. Although now that I understand why, it doesn't bother me. It took time for me to learn that Logan requires baby steps. He doesn't learn slowly, he is just a little immature and is more stubborn than a mule.

When Logan had his halo, how did this affect you? How did you feel about it? The Halo situation was quite difficult. I never understood how eight screws into Logan's head pulling out would help. It sounds like one of the torture devices in a Saw movie. I am no war hero or anything but I definitely have a little bit of PTSD. There was one morning where one of Logan's arteries had torn. I didn't know anything wrong was going on, I had just woken up and grabbed my daily bowl of cereal. To be specific it was a bowl of "Life" the day Logan almost lost his life.

I was sitting on the couch eating my cereal out of a green bowl with one of those built in straws to drink the milk. Logan came over and sat next to me after dad cleaned him up, holding his stuffed animal, which was a Beagle. As I turned to look at him, he gagged and threw up the most blood I've seen in my life. He lay there passed out and I don't remember dropping anything or stepping through blood. The only thing I can recall is sprinting to the back door and screaming at my mom, "LOGAN IS DYING LOGAN IS DYING," or something extreme. She was super stressed already knowing the situation, already being on the phone with the doctor and my memory blacks out after that.

****

I worry about Logan becoming independent, what he will do when my parents aren't around anymore, if he will meet someone that can love him for who he is, etc.

My worries have changed, and are different now compared to when I was younger. Before all I would worry about is stuff happening in the moment like his surgeries or his halo. But now, it's all about the future that worries me.

****

Do you have any advice for other siblings who have brothers or sisters with special needs? Nothing will help more in this world than reading The Holy Bible (Proverbs is great) and being patient. Another *must do,* is know that their challenges are not yours to go through, so do not make them a burden. God has given obstacles specific to you. What you go through, someone else might not be able to do, and vice versa.

****

LOGAN

What was it like having to wear the halo device screwed onto your head?

It was hard to get used to it, because it got hard to eat everyday food. I had to have liquids or it had to be something soft because I couldn't move my jaw very much. The worst part of it was only getting to have liquids.

****

What was it like having to try to sleep with the halo on?

I had to get used to it knowing that it's worth it because it would fix the issue with my brain growing faster than my skull, and so I could breathe out of my nose.

****

Did it hurt wearing it?

Sometimes it did, when we had to adjust it and manually change it over time. Sometimes turning the screws was uncomfortable.

****

How did you feel when you saw that your face had changed significantly?

It was hard for me to get used to it because it would change how people look at me.

Did you feel that after the midface advancement, it improved your appearance, or made it worse?

In a way it's in the middle between improving it and making it worse.

It's helped me do things normal people haven't. I was able to meet the manager at an exotic car dealership, so it was nice to have special treatment. Sometimes people are more generous in that way. But, it's harder to find a relationship with someone.

What are some good memories you have growing up as a kid?

I got to go to CCA retreats and see that there are other people like me. I also love family vacations.

What has helped you get through surgeries?

My family

What is the hardest part about going out in public?

People would stare.

When people stared, what would you rather them do instead of stare?

Continue with their business.

****

If you found out another child was about to go through the midface surgery and had to wear the halo for eight weeks like you did, what tips would you give them?

TIPS: try to binge watch movies.

ADVICE: that it'll be okay. Stay calm and know that they can do it.

****

Words of truth

There you have it...straight from my tribe. These were their honest thoughts and answers to the questions I thought you might like to know the answers to. I am sure there are more *wonderments*, but I felt these were pertinent questions you might be curious about.

We are all God's jars of clay, molding each differently for His purpose. We may share the same or different afflictions, each used to create a masterpiece within us (2 Corinthians 4:7-12). It's our brokenness that leads us to the ultimate creator who sacrificed His only son, so that we may have eternal life (John 3:16).

Chapter 23
One Day at a Time, Sweet Jesus

"By perseverance, the snail reached the ark."
~ *Charles Spurgeon*

Our journey continues by living the best life we can, recognizing the daily blessings upon us, and finding the joy in this journey (Philippians 4:4). Did we manage to survive challenging times in our lives and in our marriage? Yes, we did...and we still do. We now have a better understanding that life isn't about being in control one hundred percent of the time. It's about understanding that God is in control one hundred percent of the time. Ultimately, He knows and understands our needs and is always by our side through the good and bad. When we have done all we know to do in situations, whether it is decision making with all of life's changes: moving, career changing, medical decisions, financial decisions, we know we can trust God to handle the rest. Even when we *don't* know what to do in situations, we know we can trust God to lead us in the right direction, even if it means doing nothing, or staying put. He already knows the outcome, whether it is another trial or fun time ahead, yet He never waivers, and never leaves our side.

We have learned so much about prayer. Over the years *we* have prayed, *family* has prayed, and *people* whom we've never met have prayed for us...and here we are. Oh, how I believe in the power of prayer!

****

Remember the man we met at Steve's church? The one who spoke those curious words: *"you've been blessed with a test."* He passed away a few years ago, but my mother-in-law learned something extraordinary about him. She reintroduced herself to the daughter at his memorial service.

"My name is Linda, and your dad told us he prayed for our grandson Logan."

"Oh yes... *Logan.* I definitely know that name. My dad had sticky notes posted all over his house with the name Logan written on them to remind himself to pray for him," she replied.

When my mother-in-law told me this, my jaw dropped. Talk about divine intervention in action.

The test, for me, wasn't an "ah ha! In your face. Let's just see how tough you think you are, and if you're good enough to handle the task," from God. Contrarily, it was... do you trust me? Do you trust that I am here always to handle what you cannot?"

We've often heard it said, "God doesn't give us more than we can handle." Perhaps. But I also think that God helps us handle what we cannot. We live in a world where things go wrong, people get sick, or even die. For us, our first child was born with an extensive medical condition we had no knowledge of, and even the doctors were still learning from. We didn't want this for our child, Logan didn't ask, nor want this for his life, and Landon didn't want this for his brother. Yet, God knew the plan before we ever did. He knew this was going to happen. He was with us during all the hard and easy times, even when we thought He was distant, or questioned Him. It has taught me how to be more patient.

> *"Count it all joy, my brothers, when you meet trials of various kinds, for you know that the testing of your faith produces steadfastness." ~ James 1:2-3.*

****

Our hard times haven't magically disappeared, but over time they seem to become less and farther between now that Logan is an adult, which leads to new worries. God has always given whatever it was we needed at the time, whether it was discernment, courage, strength or patience, and I'm so thankful (Philippians 4:11-13). Heck, there was even a time we were so financially strapped after Logan was born, and we had bills we weren't able to pay. I frantically worried about what we would do, and was too proud to say anything to anyone, or ask for money. The same week, Steve's mom called me and said her Sunday school class had been praying for us, and took up a collection of a little over $200, and she dropped it in the mail for us. I was overwhelmed, because it was about how much we needed to pay the bills. Coincidence? I think not.

There was a long period of time when Steve and I tried to mend the wounds that seemed to stay open in our hearts, no matter what we did. We were both hurting, but I don't think we knew *how* to help each other. Our focus was always on Logan… rarely each other. We forgot to take care of *each other.* Satan's lie told us we were alone and weak if we weren't in control of every situation.

At times, we fell prey to the belief that we had to handle everything on our own, and it almost destroyed our marriage.

Of course, we still have worries. We're human. It takes so much of our mental and emotional energy when we worry, that it so often blinds us from our everyday blessings. Learning to manage anxieties and trust God has been the ultimate gift (Matthew 6:25-34).

I'm also thankful for the times we *weren't* given what we thought was best at the time. There were so many times when it seemed God was distant during our many tests and trials. We had a notion we would move across two states to the northwest of where we were, but we didn't...our house sat on the market for a year and a half with hundreds of lookers, but no buyers. Why? It wasn't God's plan for us.

He told us *no*. I didn't understand it at the time, and felt quite frustrated. Would I have liked to live closer to my sister? Absolutely. She is my left hand, my best friend and confidante. Yet, God knew we still had things to do where we were. Logan still had numerous surgeries ahead of him, and we were only two hours from the hospital. If we had moved to Wyoming, we would have been 1,900 miles away.

I also thought I was going to be an educational diagnostician, but that didn't pan out either. God wanted me to remain in the classroom, teaching children with special needs, and also learning from them. I remained in education for sixteen years, until God called me to write. Never in a million years would I have thought I would be writing and sharing about our intimate and personal experiences. If I hadn't pursued my master's degree in special education with all of the written papers required, I probably never would have written this book. I might have tried, but mostly likely would have given up.

I'm glad He's told me no in some circumstances. Despite the hardships, changes, tears and tireless work, I can't imagine my life being different now. Even though He said *no* then, it was because He had a better *yes* for our future.

What about those times when Logan was so close to death? Why were *we* the lucky ones to not lose our child? I am so grateful to God for sparing his life, because after his bleeding episode, he shouldn't be alive today, logic doesn't prove it. Yet, he is still here with us. I often go through bouts of survivor's guilt, knowing there have been many parents who've lost their child. I can't even begin to imagine the depths of despair they must have, and still feel. Why were *we* so lucky? Our time on earth is unknown, but the best way I know how to serve God through all of this, is to share Him with you.

Remember the sweet young lady who knelt down in front of me, offering her words of encouragement and prayers? The one who bought Logan his first stuffed toy, the puppy named Rescue, which did rescue him from many days and nights of fear and pain? With the help of another *cranio mom*, as I call my connections, we found her on social media. In a time of need, this stranger gave me a divine message of hope. I took some time to gather my thoughts before I reached out to her. I wanted her to know how much her words meant to me, to my family, and how special Rescue was to our son, and her words were not in vain. This was the letter I wrote:

November 28, 2018

Dear XXXX,

My name is Lisa Brown and I live in Texas. I am married to Steve and we have two sons, Logan (17 years old) and Landon (13 years old).

We don't really know each other, and you may not remember me, but we met seventeen years ago at Medical City Dallas Hospital.

You made a huge impact on my life seventeen years ago, which convicted me to reach out to you. I gave birth to my first son Logan on January 18, 2002. We received a diagnosis for him of Apert Syndrome two days later. His skull fusion was very severe, and it was recommended that he have surgery right away, so he had his first cranial vault when he was twelve days old, on January 30, 2002.

While we were waiting in the small surgery waiting room, you walked in and introduced yourself. Your husband was just outside the waiting room holding your daughter. I believe her name is Saige. She had her Lefort III (halo) attached, and if my memory serves me correctly, you were being discharged at that time, getting ready to head back home, I don't believe you lived in Texas.

I am writing to you because you really made an impression on me seventeen years ago, and I have never forgotten you.

I was completely distraught at the time, as we were still trying to wrap our minds around the new diagnosis that we had never heard of, much less deal with the grueling surgery our son was going through.

After you had introduced yourself to me, you knelt down on your knees in front of where I was sitting, looked me straight in the eyes, and with such a calm and reassuring voice said, "God is going to take care of your little boy, and you and your husband."

You gave me words that I desperately needed to hear, especially from someone who was going through the same thing that Steve and I were. You had given us your number and email at the time (since back then there was no social media), but somewhere along the way, it got lost in our transition home after being discharged. You and your husband even left a card in his PICU room, as well as a plush little puppy with balloons around his neck. I'm not sure if the puppy was from you or not, but if it was, that was a blessing! My son carried it around with him everywhere he went, and he slept with it until he was finally too old for it. Now it sits in his keepsake box.

I have thought about you and your family often over these years, and since I had lost the piece of paper you gave me with your information on it, I couldn't remember your full name.

In 2017, I met with another friend who lives in Dallas, her son has Crouzon's Syndrome and we have become good friends. I mentioned you to her, and how I wished I could remember your name, and she told me she thought I must be talking about you.

As soon as I looked you up on Facebook, I knew it was you when I saw your face.

All this to say...I wanted to tell you how much I appreciated your kind words for me during such a difficult time. It took me a long time to reach out to others in the craniofacial world, but once I did, I found myself wanting to comfort and encourage others just as much as you did for me years ago.

I firmly believe that God places people in our lives in His perfect timing, even if it is only for a brief moment.

Thank you so much for your warmth and kindness. Please look me up on social media sometime, or feel free to email or text me, I would love to connect with you someday. I am listing all of my social media and blog sites. I actually started blogging about four years ago, with hopes of encouraging others. I have also discovered that writing is helpful and therapeutic for me :)

Website: lisadbrown.com
Facebook Blog Page: **One Real Hero** *(this is where I post about Logan's updates)*
Facebook Blog Page (2): **Lisa D Brown @lisadbrownauthor**
Instagram: **@lisadbrownauthor**
Twitter: **@lisadbauthor**

God Bless,
Lisa Brown

When she responded to my letter, she said she remembered me and asked how Logan was doing. I was devastated to find out that her daughter had passed away. I sat with my thoughts and emotions after learning this news. Initially, I was upset, and a little angry for *her*. She is the one who told me God was going to take care of our child and get us through this. Little did she know that she would lose hers. Survivor's guilt pressed at my temple again, until I scrolled through her Facebook page. I saw happy pictures of her family that had grown with a son and an adopted girl. My instinct was to ask God why she lost her daughter who had Apert, but I am reminded that her story, her purpose, her lesson, isn't the same as mine. Yet, with her act of compassion, she certainly ministered to my family and me, which has made all the difference. So, her daughter's legacy lives on.

We exchanged family stories and updates, and I could tell she has a happy life now. She misses her daughter immensely which makes her ache even more for heaven, but knows she is waiting for her up in heaven. I was relieved to know that she is at peace now after losing her. She is devoted to God and her family and it was clear that she understands her purpose in life.

God puts people in our lives on purpose, at times it may be obvious to us, but often it may be to carry out a brand new, glorious plan He lays out in our path.

I worked in a school district with leaders unafraid to pray for their staff. All the teachers I worked with in my last eight years of teaching prayed for our family every time Logan had surgery. God knew that in order for me to be able to go back to work to teach my students with special needs, that I needed to be surrounded by people who would lift up my family.

Even with indistinguishable circumstances, we all still have different journeys and purposes for what we go through in our lives. Over the past ten years I've met and connected with hundreds of families with a child who has Apert Syndrome, or other craniofacial syndromes. Most of us have experienced medical traumas alike and can bond in this way. However, even with the same diagnosis, each family's experience will be unique:

- Some experience medical complications, some do not, or their complications are completely different from others.
- Some have to travel hundreds, even thousands, of miles for their medical care, others do not.
- Some have great social experiences, while others may feel isolated, alone, or deal with bullying.
- Some accompany more diagnoses aside from Apert Syndrome, but others may not.

This list could go on.

For Logan, no matter the challenge, he *eventually* adapted, or overcame.

Some similarities to what we go through on this journey with Apert Syndrome, doesn't change the fact that God has a different plan for each and every one of us. His timing is perfect, not ours. I recognize, and appreciate now, that God has control and I don't. "But we have this treasure in jars of clay, to show that the surpassing power belongs to God and not us. We are afflicted in every way, but not crushed; perplexed, but not driven to despair; persecuted, but not forsaken; struck down, but not destroyed." (2 Corinthians 4:7-9, ESV).

If there is anything I would share with other parents of kids with special needs, it would be to celebrate the little things. I would remind them to stop and reflect on how their child was doing five years ago, or maybe 10 years ago. Are they reaching a milestone they never knew if they would? Or, maybe they are finally able to go out in public without melting into sensory overload. Can you look back and now say that they can hold their head up on their own when you wondered and dreamed if they ever would? There are so many skills we take for granted until we see our children struggle with them. As parents, it's difficult because we want our children to succeed and live happy lives.

It has been a blessing to have social media, providing connections that never would have been made without it. But, like anything involving the public, evil can and will reap its head by using those who are vulnerable to troll into shame. While cautiously protective, we must still continue with our journey God has given us. Fight the good fight, and battle fear with faith and hope. Don't let the enemy tell you who you should or shouldn't be, or give you worldly expectations to live up to, because you will fail every time. God knows who we are, and with Him, we are all we need to be.

I truly believe there are still great people in our world, ones who acknowledge, include, serve and love one another for the good cause. Unfortunately, the evil sometimes gets the better of our attention, but we must keep going. No matter what you've been through, or what kind of walk you are on in your journey, God still has plans for good in our lives (Jeremiah 29:11). You can choose to "Own your story. You don't have to like all of it, but allow God to use you to help others" (Lisa D Brown, 2020).

If we are alive and still breathing, we still have purpose. Hard times are inevitable and will still come, but having a relationship with Jesus and putting trust in Him has been a game changer for me. Have conversations with Jesus. Just like our parents (and if you are a parent you may feel this same way), He wants us to come to Him when we're angry, frustrated, anxious, sad, but also joyful when we are aware and acknowledge that He never leaves our side.

None of us know what is in store for tomorrow, and we may encounter more *unexpected* adventures. Only God knows. The best part is that God is always with us, through thick and thin, through His son Jesus. He will be there to celebrate our joy, hold us during our sorrow and grief, and lift us out of the darkness. He also rejoices and celebrates with us during our happy times when we acknowledge that our blessings come from Him. I have the knowledge and faith that I don't have to handle every burden on my own. Most importantly, my family has a relationship with Jesus.

Days will not always be easy, and I know there are new chapters in our lives, and there may still be sufferings ahead. I know God will get us through anything, and find those disguised blessings through our sufferings (Romans 5:2-5).

Memories still flood my soul, and we still work through the aftermath of trauma. In no way am I comparing it to war veterans, but medical trauma is real. I didn't always want to deal with my feelings because it was too hard, too painful. Many times I avoided them intentionally, but other times were out of my control because I didn't have time, and had to keep the family going. When the dust settles, that bitterness that is still pinned up inside you will crawl out of you like a creature from a science fiction movie…and when you least expect it. I've learned through experience though, it's okay to go sit in your closet, bathtub, car, or wherever you can have a few minutes alone and just…cry…wail the ugly cry. Scream into the pillow if you have to. Dealing is healing. The way *we* heal is through conversations, and the more we have them, another link from the shackle is detached. Not everyone will understand what it's like, and that's okay. Some expect you to just "get over it and move on." Grief is a cycle, and the ebbs and flows will thwart its way to you when you don't expect it. There have been times when I experience certain sights, sounds, and smells that suck me straight back to those hospital days. Some are unpleasant, but others aren't so bad. They remind me of where we've been, what we've been through, and where we are now in life.

There is a post office atrium that smells exactly like the clean, sterile, hospital blankets and sheets. A few department stores use the same soap in their bathroom as the ones in the public bathrooms at the hospital. I've heard noises that sound like the cadence of the hospital monitor machines. They're repulsive and stop me in my tracks. When I see an ambulance, I say a quick prayer for those involved.

In the beginning, these memories were difficult to face since they reminded me of how hard times have been. They brought back dark and lonely feelings. But now, they only remind me of how blessed we are *because* of those hard times, and how we have triumphed. I have a close relationship with God now, and I know that I must turn to Him for answers. We may get sucked back to past memories from time to time, but we don't allow feelings of despair weigh us down. Instead, our talks about the past let the memories show us where we've been, and how God pulled us through. Our scars, whether visible or not, are proof that we've endured. They remind us of how much God loves, and still has purpose for us.

After Logan had his last annual checkup with the surgeon, the doctor recommended that he come back when he turns 21 to do an updated MRI and sleep study. He is most likely done with major surgeries, unless an urgent concern arises, but the doctor said he wants to continue checkups every few years because they are still learning and researching more about Apert Syndrome.

We walked downstairs, down the hallway to the main lobby in building A. We passed the shoeshine stand and it occurred to me that I never see the shoeshine guy there anymore. I wonder what happened to him. Did he pass away, or does he not work here anymore? The carousel has now been remodeled, so the animals look renewed, even more vibrant and alive than they used to be. The long runway I used to stare at on the old carpet pattern is gone, but there's new, fresh carpet now. It's how God works in us as well. Out with the old, in with the new. He refreshes our soul, wants us to not strain too hard at what once was, but look forward and strive ahead to what is now, and what's to come (Philippians, 3:12-14).

Before we left, we stopped at the smoothie bar and ordered some for our ride home. I asked Logan if we could sit on the benches by the waterfall for just a minute. My heart twisted with nostalgia. Fifty percent of his childhood was in this hospital…fifty percent of my motherhood was too. Memories confiscated me, playing a projector of video in my mind of the first time I held Logan by these water fountains at only ten days old. I think of the gift shop to our right where my mother-in-law bought Logan a toddler size helium balloon of Elmo. I think of the numerous times we ate at the cafeteria and different eateries. Eighteen years and fifteen surgeries later, I was sitting next to him as an adult, drinking a smoothie. So much has changed, and oh how grateful I am!

Logan graduated high school and is ready for his adulthood to begin…freedom. Frankly, he (we) thought school would never end; at least it felt that way. His whole life he had been held down for needles, forced to have surgeries, and all the things he didn't ask for…yet, he endured.

Landon survived his freshman year of high school and is doing well with baseball and his love of animals. He was always precocious growing up, and now he disciples to his peers, so I know God has big plans for him.

I reminisce through all the emotions I've felt over the years through this ordeal. *Man, we've been through the ringer over the years, but oh how we've had so many good times, memories, and experiences.* I've found joy in this journey, and that is because Jesus gave it to me. He gives me blessings and guides me through the hard times. He placed people in our lives when we needed them; gave us extraordinary surgeons; friends that were always there for us; a loving pastor and church family who loves us as their *own* family members; and family who never left our sides. While hardships took place in our story, *this* is a journey of blessings.

Change is inevitable, and life *is* change, but God remains the same yesterday, today, and forever (Hebrews 13:8). I've learned so much from reading my bible and attending a wonderful church with some pretty awesome people. When things feel scary and unpredictable, first, I talk it over with God. Then, I allow the words my sweet grandma would say, resonate with me while they lead me through each day...*One day at a time, sweet Jesus.*

****

"Now may the Lord of peace himself give you peace at all times and in every way. The Lord be with you all."

~ 2 Thessalonians 3:16

Changing *Faces*

Logan & Dr. Jeffrey Fearon

Acknowledgements

When I thought about this final day of writing my acknowledgements page, I wondered how on earth I would be able to thank so many people who have played a role in our lives through this journey. So, I'll just allow the Holy Spirit to guide me.

First, I want to say thank you to Logan for allowing me to share our story. Thank you for showing me what the true meaning of perseverance is. God chose me to be your mom, and I am a better person because of you, and I am so grateful!

Steve, thank you for believing in me. Although it took several years for this to come to fruition, you never waivered your faith in me, and faith that God would keep His promise and see it through. Thank you for your devotion to our family by providing a good life and working so hard. I know it hasn't been easy. Landon, you have a servant's heart and I've known this since you were little. You watched and observed, and have been your brother's keeper all these years. You knew more medical terms at a young age than most adults. Thank you for teaching me how to laugh again. Your gregarious personality cannot be matched. Your thirst for God is a true calling, and I cannot wait to watch you grow your ministry in the years to come.

Emmett and Linda Hartsfield, my parents, thank you for always being there for me. You have loved and supported me through many life decisions - good ones, and a few dumb ones. But I've always felt your love and knew I could come to you no matter what, and *that* is the ultimate gift a parent can give. Thank you for being such wonderful grandparents to my boys! I love you both so much.

To my in-laws, Walter and Linda Brown, your love and dedication to our family is a true example of God's love. Thank you for always being there for us, and especially for raising your son in Christ. Thanks to the late Aunt Ginna for the beautiful poem.

Lori, your are my beloved sister. I could write another chapter on how much I want to say to you. You are my best friend…my confidant…my shoulder to cry on. You've been my sounding board through this whole writing process, and your opinion means the world to me! I don't know what I would do without having you with me through this, not only making sure I remain on the mark of sanity, but always being the one who laughs with me at the silly stuff in life. I love you dearly sister! Tony, my brother, luckily you are the "smart" one in the family and already had so much knowledge with that peculiar network, back then they called…the internet. You didn't hesitate to put your skills to work to find some answers for us. Thank you and I love you.

My pastor, my brother in Christ, my friend…Donnie Foster, thank you for encouraging me and holding me accountable before God to see this through. I'm so grateful to you, Karen, and your family for pouring into our family with love and being there for us!

Thank you to the late Dr. Kenneth Salyer, Logan's first cranial surgeon. Your dedication to helping children with craniofacial differences was a true legacy. Your special hands worked so many miracles.

Dr. Fearon, as I've heard you tell Logan before, you've both "grown up together." I am so glad we found you. The care you provide Logan either during an appointment or on your operating table is as if he were your own son, and it makes all the difference. This is a cherished quality we love you for!

How do I even begin to name all the educators, staff, and administrators in our school district who guided Logan during this journey? You took on these roles as his proponent in education with compassion and kindness. Thanks to all my former coworkers at Fine

Arts Academy for making his elementary years a positive experience. Lisa Brannon, you will always have a special place in my heart, and Logan's. You were his greatest teacher of all, for so many years, and you were willing to *step outside of the box* for him. To all the ladies at First Class Learning Center (past and present), you mean the world to me. Each day you gave me peace when I had to leave my own children so that I could work. Knowing that my children were in such a safe and loving environment meant the world to me. Thank you Frank Molinar, for your leadership, and making children a priority. Desiree Coyle, you are passionate and on fire for kids. I'm so grateful for you. Thank you for listening, believing, and bringing life to my "choose kind" mission.

To our dear friends Heather, and Lanham Stark... Heather, thank you for being my friend during my months (perhaps year) of *madness* when I needed someone to hear me. Even though you took on my stress as it was your own, you stuck by my side so I always had a place to fall. Through my healing, I can now imagine how hard it was to see a friend suffer, and most often not know what to say. I've learned from other "cranio" families that some friends *disappear.* Thank you for not disappearing during my most vulnerable times. Lanham, you're an upstanding citizen, ex-neighbor, and friend. Thank you for being there for us as well. I don't know what we would have done on *that day,* had you not been taking out the trash. I am forever grateful for you both and love you.

Heather Williams, you are another treasure God put in my path during my years of teaching. Not only were you the best inclusive P.E. teacher I've ever known, but you are my sister in Christ who modeled prayer for me. Fond memories of our few ghost hunting girls' trips with you and Heather Stark, remind me of the laughter we shared. I desperately needed it and it helped me feel normal again. From the bottom of my heart, thank you for the time both of you came over to clean my house while we were in the hospital with Logan. You knew that my shoulders couldn't take one more straw of weight, so you stepped in and took care of things.

Especially thanks to my sweet editor Billye Johnson. Your professional eloquence is sincere. I appreciate your help in bringing this project to life.

Jodi Thompson, it's amazing how one connection can lead to so many doors opening! Words aren't enough to express my gratitude to you for taking the time from your busy schedule to beta read for this newbie writer.

Heather "Doc" Miller, you are my 'ya-ya' sister, my travel buddy, and I love you with all of my heart. I'm so glad God "crossed" our paths and we became friends. Thank you for encouraging me to the finish line…I made it!

A special thanks to Carie Magee with Monkey House Photography for allowing me to use the beautiful moments she captured of my family and me.

Thank you Angela Hoy with Abuzz Press for taking a chance on me!

April B. I hope you know how much it meant to me on that fateful day, when you took the time to spend ten minutes with a total stranger in a waiting room, to give her the encouragement she needed. Your sweet angel is flying high above in Heaven with wings of a dove, watching over you and anticipating your reunion some day.

Lastly, but certainly not least, to my one and only savior, Jesus. This story never would have been written without His spirit within me. He is my redeemer, my savior, and my father in Heaven who loves me always, no matter what, and gives me strength everyday.

Notes

Chapter 1

1. "Courage is not simply one of the virtues, but the form of every virtue at the testing point." ~ C.S. Lewis,
https://www.brainyquote.com/quotes/c_s_lewis_100842

Chapter 2

1. "Never be afraid to trust an unknown future to a known God." ~ Corrie Ten Boom,
https://parade.com/973277/jessicasager/inspirational-quotes/

Chapter 3

1. "Your most profound and intimate experiences of worship will likely be in your darkest days-when your heart is broken, when you feel abandoned, when you're out of options, when the pain is great-and you turn to God alone." - Rick Warren; Rick Warren, Purpose Driven Life. (Grand Rapids: Zondervan, 2002), 194.

Chapter 4

1. "I sustain myself with the love of family." ~Maya Angelo,
https://www.azquotes.com/quote/350299
2. https://en.m.wikipedia.org/wiki/Eug%C3%A8ne_Apert (Eugene Apert).
3. See Philippians 4:6-7.

Chapter 5

1. Loggins, Kenny. "Rainbow Connection." *Return to Pooh Corner.* Sony Music Entertainment, 1994. CD.

Chapter 6

1. See 1 Peter 4:12-14

2.   Dr. Jeffrey Fearon;
http://thecraniofacialcenter.com/meet_dr_fearon.html

Chapter 7

1.   *"If you can't fly then run, if you can't run then walk, if you can't walk then crawl, but whatever you do you have to keep moving forward." ~Martin Luther King Jr.,* https://literarydevices.net/if-you-cant-fly-then-run/

Chapter 8

1.   *"Yesterday is history, tomorrow is a mystery, today is a gift of God, which is why we call it the present." -Bil Keane,* https://quotes.thefamouspeople.com/bil-keane-845.php

2.   *Children's Craniofacial Association;* https://ccakids.org

3.   War. "Low Rider." *Why Can't We Be Friends?* Far Out Productions, Inc.; Rhino Entertainment Company: a Warner Music Group Company. 1975.

Chapter 9

1.   "Tis true my form is something odd, but blaming me is blaming God..."
~ Isaac Watts, https://www.goodreads.com/quotes/405059-tis-true-my-form-is-something-odd-but-blaming-me

2.   See Nehemiah 9:7-38

Chapter 10

1. "When one door of happiness closes, another opens; but often we look so long at the closed door that we do not see the one which has been opened for us." -Helen Keller,
https://www.goodreads.com/quotes/3443-when-one-door-of-happiness-closes-another-opens-but-often

Chapter 11

1. "You can't steal second base and keep one foot on first." - Frederick B. Wilcox, https://institutesuccess.com/library/progress-always-involves-risks-you-cant-steal-second-base-and-keep-your-foot-on-first-frederick-b-wilcox/

Chapter 14

1. "I wish everyday could be Halloween. We could all wear masks all the time. Then we could walk around and get to know each other before we got to see what we looked like under the masks." ~Auggie from "Wonder," by R.J. Palacio; Wonder. (New York, Alfred A. Knopf, an imprint of Random House Children's Books, 2012).

Chapter 15

1. "Everybody is a genius. But if you judge a fish by its ability to climb a tree, it will live its whole life believing that it is stupid." ~ Albert Einstein, https://www.azquotes.com/quote/369274
2. The Journey Church; http://journey-church.com/

Chapter 16

1. See Romans 12:12

Chapter 17

1. *"Who sees the human face correctly: the photographer, the mirror, or the painter?"* ~ *Pablo Picasso,* https://www.azquotes.com/quote/231337
2. See Psalm 30:5

Chapter 18

1. See John 16:33
2.

Chapter 20

1. *"The most difficult thing is the decision to act. The rest is merely tenacity." ~ Amelia Earhart, https://www.azquotes.com/quote/85081*
2. WSISD Choose Kind YouTube Video; *https://www.youtube.com/watch?v=5sFHLSb4ubI)*
3. See Ephesians 6:13-18
4. See Ephesians 5:2
5. See Jeremiah 29:11

Chapter 21

1. Life Is (modified version), https://www.poemhunter.com/poem/life-is-a-challenge-4/
2. See Philippian 3:12-14

Chapter 22

1. *"Shared stories build a relational bridge that Jesus can walk across from your hearts to others." ~Rick Warren,* Rick Warren, *Purpose Driven Life. (Grand Rapids: Zondervan, 2002), 290.*
2. See 2 Corinthians 4:7-12
3. See John 3:16

Chapter 23

1. *"By perseverance, the snail reached the ark." ~ Charles Spurgeon,*

https://www.brainyquote.com/quotes/charles_spurgeon_143068

2. See Philippians 4:4

3. See Philippians 4:11-13

4. See Matthew 6:25-34

5. One Real Hero website; http://onerealhero.blogspot.com/

6. See James 1:2-3

7. Lisa D Brown website; https://www.lisadbrown.com/; Social Media: *Facebook Blog Page (2):* Lisa D Brown @lisadbrownauthor; *Instagram*: **@lisadbrownauthor;** *Twitter:* **@lisadbauthor**

8. See 2 Corinthians 4:7-9

9. See Jeremiah 29:11

10. See Romans 5:2-5

11. See Philippians, 3:12-14

12. See Hebrews 13:8

13. "Now may the Lord of peace himself give you peace at all times and in every way. The Lord be with you all." ~ 2 Thessalonians 3:16

Information & Resources

- ❖ The Craniofacial Center - Dallas, Texas, USA; http://thecraniofacialcenter.com/index.html
- ❖ Apert International, Inc.; https://www.apert-international.org/
- ❖ Apert Owl – Outreach With Love; https://www.apertowl.org/
- ❖ FACES – National Craniofacial Association; https://www.faces-cranio.org/
- ❖ World Craniofacial Foundation; https://worldcf.org/
- ❖ American Society of Craniofacial Surgeons; https://ascfs.org/
- ❖ Children's Craniofacial Association; https://ccakids.org/
- ❖ Knit For a Unique Fit – Facebook group for custom made gloves; https://www.facebook.com/groups/968877786968046/
- ❖ Look At Us; https://lookatus.org/

About the Author

Lisa is a native Texan where she lives with her husband, two sons, three dogs, and ten chickens. She taught elementary special education for sixteen years, and now works part time in accounting. Lisa began blogging after her oldest son's multiple surgeries to share his progress with family and friends. She extended her writing focus to encourage and inspire other families raising children with disabilities. Besides writing, Lisa serves as a ladies' ministry leader and disciple maker in her church. She enjoys reading, traveling, gardening, crocheting, watching Friends reruns, and true crime documentaries.

www.ingramcontent.com/pod-product-compliance
Lightning Source LLC
Chambersburg PA
CBHW032004150726
47990CB00005B/1830